Developing and Managing
Organizational Learning

AMERICAN SOCIETY FOR TRAINING & DEVELOPMENT

Developing
and Managing
Organizational
Learning

KAREN OVERFIELD

A Guide to Effective
Training Project Management

Ordering information: Books published by the American Society for Training & Development can be ordered by calling 800.628.2783 or 703.683.8100.

Library of Congress Catalog Card Number: 98-73225
ISBN: 1-56286-090-9

Table of Contents

1. Developing and Managing Training Programs..1

2. Training Program Management...15

3. Step 1: Present/Future State Analysis..37

4. Step 2: Program Design...47

5. Step 3: Research...59

6. Step 4: Resource Allocation 73

7. Step 5: Instructional Design 81

8. Step 6: Training Program Instructional Development.........................91

9. Step 7: Training Program Implementation 103

10. Training Program Evaluation..125

11. Summary 135

References...139

Other Resources..140

The Author 147

1

Developing and Managing Training Programs

Role of Training and Development in Traditional Organizations

To succeed in a competitive environment, organizations need skilled workers, and for these employees to stay current and update their skills, they need training. Intuitively, management knows that workers develop greater efficiencies through focused training events than from on-the-job work, which produces only accidental skill development.

At one time, organizations viewed training and development as a means for building employee loyalty and "growing their own." These companies established defined career paths and linked training to advancement. Whether employees needed the training or not, they went through it because attendance was a prerequisite for advancement. Employees in some companies thought of courses as punches in a card that would enable them to climb the corporate ladder, like the 10 punches on a card some restaurants require before patrons get a free dinner.

Organizations viewed employee training and development as one of management's responsibilities and held human resource development (HRD) functions accountable for delivering it. Corporate universities became a source of pride for the organization and a way to build loyalty in those people who were sent to them. Employees viewed training and development as both a reward for good work and an entitlement.

Role of Training in the Learning Organization

In the past few years, the words *training and development* have taken on new connotations. Organizations have reinvented themselves and in this process have taken a closer look at their unwritten contracts with their employees. Many organizations that took pride in their low employee turnover and in their reputations as lifelong employers now embrace employment at will. These organizations view the new contract as a fair day's wages for a fair day's work. Instead of developing people to climb career ladders, they provide employees with marketable skills for transportable careers. Few employees spend their entire career with one organization. Advancement means changing organizations, careers, and locations, not just getting a promotion.

Over the years, a shift has also occurred in companies' training philosophies. Organizations once provided training to help individual employees become better contributors to the organization. As organizations began to embrace total quality management, however, they began to recognize the role of intact work groups. Training became focused on those groups so they could function better as teams. Today, organizations reengineer for a holistic, systemic view and focus on process rather than functions. They strive to become learning organizations in which learning is captured within the organization and the whole organization learns. *Learning* becomes synonymous with work. Although training and development may look different from the way they used to look, the value added to the organization remains. In today's organizations, competitive advantage lies in employees' skills, knowledge, and abilities. The opportunity to learn new skills, grow on the job, and keep skills marketable represents both the competitive advantage for the organization and the vehicle with which to attract and keep valued employees.

To manage training in the learning organization, employees who plan training programs need to consider both internal and external factors. External factors include governmental regulations, societal forces, market, economy, philosophies, and laws. Internal factors include resources—time, money, staff—culture, and learners.

This book provides the employees who plan programs and those who provide training with a tool kit with which to lead learning in their organization. Organizations often criticize training program planning for a lack of rigor and methodology and fault program planners for a lack of business skills. The tools presented in this book overcome those problems by linking program planning to project management. By using these additional skills, program planners lead program planning as a project, demonstrate critical thinking skills, and develop skills in decision making, which enable them to complete programs on time and within budget. The skills, knowledge, and abilities the program planner learns to use are transportable and applicable to all types of projects. Thus, as the program planner learns, the organization captures this learning so it can use the planning and implementation process for other events.

By using this book's tool kit, employees can shift their roles from that of training program planner to training project manager. Readers will notice that this book refers to those employees as training program planners at first and then as training project managers to reflect the changed role. The experience and skill levels training project managers gain provide them with marketable abilities that they can apply to manage other types of projects.

Reasons for Growth of Training and Development

Organizations spend over $56 billion each year on employee training and development programs. The training field represents a billion-dollar industry within the United States, one that continues to grow. Why? Several of the reasons include

- **Constantly changing environment.** As Kotter (1997) states in *Leading Change*:

  The change problem inside organizations would become less worrisome if the business environment would soon stabilize or at least slow down. But most credible evidence suggests the opposite: that the rate of environmental movement will increase and that the pressures on organizations to transform themselves will grow over the next few decades.

- **Marketplace ratcheted up competition.** Businesses find themselves in a global market, rather than a local, regional, or national market. Ease of information exchange, advances in technology, and speed of delivery enable organizations to compete in the global market.

A shift has taken place in the focus for competitive advantage. Manufacturers received payback on the technological advances made in production lines; now they are looking for returns from workers and high-performance work systems. Organizations find that they must gain the competitive advantage through the creation of high-performance work systems and employee performance management systems.

- **Permutations in the psychological contract between worker and organization.** Not so long ago, employees joined an organization and proceeded up a recognized career ladder. In return, employers got a loyal and stable workforce. Now, careers represent winding paths rather than vertical ladders. In today's psychological contract, employees get a marketable set of skills to make their careers transportable. For career advancement and continued employment, employees switch organizations. Employers benefit from employees' advanced skills during the time of employment. They gain flexibility to change the makeup of their workforce as their needs evolve.

- **Lifelong learning a reality for workers.** During the past few years, the half-life of a college education decreased from 10 years to five; in technical areas, it's as short as six months. With employees' need to update their skills constantly, training and development programs become critical to organizations' success. In our dynamic work environment, employees find they need to train, retrain, or enhance their skills, and employers must offer continued professional development for competitive advantages. Each party holds a responsibility for training and development: one to provide an environment conducive for learning, and the other, to learn. Successful organizations transform into learning organizations built on a culture of learning.

Administration of Training and Development

Traditionally, an organization's human resource development, organizational development, or training and development department delivered, coordinated, and administered programs. The professionals in these areas designed programs or purchased off-the-shelf courses to meet their organization's requirements.

Training was reactive rather than proactive in the past. Departments published elaborate catalogs, schedules, and communications to support, market, and advertise their programs, and organizations viewed training as discrete activities. Training departments counted the number of people trained, courses delivered, and hours attended as measurements of their achievements. Training costs and savings got measured through reports showing contact hours, decreased expenses related to training, reduction in no-shows to the courses, and increased room utilization.

Trainers didn't form partnerships with line management. Management sent the departments their problems to be "fixed," employees saw the programs as those punches on a card to career advancement, and people attended the flavor-of-the-year program. Organizations viewed training as a panacea to fix performance problems. When training didn't fix the problem, management judged the training as bad.

In "Seven Ways to Make Your Training Department One of the Best," Vander Linde, Harney, and Koonce (August 1997) state the following:

> In traditional organizations, training often operates as a staff function separate from line operations and without performance metrics to assess quantitatively whether the training produces results in terms of organizational goals and plans. Typically, training in such organizations has limited customer focus (for example, a classroom of participants). Satisfaction measurements tend to be event-based (for example, course evaluation forms) rather than continuous and organizational.

Transformational organizations—those that recreate themselves as learning organizations—take a proactive approach to training. The role of the trainer has evolved into that of a change agent in which trainers develop collaborative partnerships with line management. Training has become seamless with the job, not an isolated event. The focus of training has moved away from an individual contributor and to the organization. With this shift in focus, the organization itself learns as well as its employees.

John Redding (1997) categorizes the learning organization this way:

- Organizations and groups, not just individuals learn

- The degree that an organization learns determines its capability to transform itself to meet demands for fast, fundamental change

- A company is a learning organization to the degree that it has purposefully built its capacity to learn as a whole system and woven that capacity into all of its aspects: vision and strategy, leadership and management, culture, structure, systems, and processes.

In such an organization, training's role changes. Trainers share responsibility for job performance with line management. A trainer moves from being a professional in the delivery of training events to becoming a performance consultant, and this consultant's role evolves from that of a pair of hands, or expert, to that of a collaborator, a partner with line management. Because performance is one of the trainer's responsibilities, training can't be the only tool in the trainer's tool chest. Training must incorporate performance improvement interventions as well. When it does, training's emphasis matures into human performance improvement in the workplace.

When to Train

Organizations can benefit from providing both proactive and reactive training for their people. They benefit through the increased performance of their workers. Organizations need to keep in mind that they should use training to address performance issues. Examples of when organizations should train include the following:

- **To facilitate people's learning of new systems, equipment, processes, and procedures.** When organizations implement new systems, equipment, processes, and procedures, they face the choice of expecting their employees to learn informally on their own or providing them with structured training sessions. Typically, an organization will spend hundreds of thousand of dollars for new equipment and then not train its people. The organization then wonders why it did not realize the benefits the vendor promised. Rothwell and Cookson (1997) state that

> Informal learning is, however, notoriously inefficient and time-consuming. It is rarely sufficient to help adults meet the challenges of changing work requirements. Moreover, many workers resent being thrust into sink-or-swim experiences without prior learning. For these reasons, organizations sponsor planned programs to support, facilitate, and accelerate work performance mastery and improve the ability of its [*sic*] workforce to meet or exceed customer requirements.

- **To provide developmental opportunity for employees.** Organizations tend to identify excellent performers and recognize them by giving them a different job assignment. The organization assumes that an employee who did well in one situation will do well in another, although the employee may enter the "new" assignment without any prior experience or learning. When this happens, the organization sets the employee up for failure.

  Ideally, the employees slated for advancement or job enrichment should get an opportunity for a developmental learning experience prior to assuming the new work situation. This experience can come in the form of training, mentoring, or a temporary assignment. By participating in this type of developmental experience, the employee gains the chance to make mistakes, practice skills, and enhance abilities in a less-threatening environment before being assessed on the job. The organization reduces the person's learning curve on the job, chance of making a costly mistake, and likelihood to fail.

- **Resolve identified performance problems of workers.** Typically, the first thought of a supervisor who notices a problem with a worker's performance is to send the worker to a training session. This is probably the most common reason for training. Unfortunately, it is also the most abused.

Before taking steps to correct a problem, however, trainers and line management must decide together if the problem is a training related one. Training is an expensive solution, particularly if the problem isn't a training one. Training fills a specific need—to provide workers with the skills they need to do their job. Training events take time to design, develop, and deliver. Key questions that need to be asked before starting a training program include

- What is the problem?

- Does the problem need to be fixed?

- Could the worker do the job if his or her life depended on it?

- How can I best solve the problem?

Figure 1 contains a simple diagnostic tool to use to help answer the question, Is it a training problem? Consider an employee with a performance problem and place an *X* in the spot where that person fits in the grid. If your employee has low motivation and low job knowledge, for example, the person would fit into quadrant A. Does that employee need training? Probably not. Would training "fix" the performance problem? I doubt it.

Figure 1. A diagnostic tool to identify training problems.

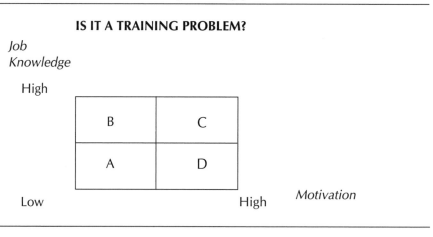

That employee might be in the wrong job, in denial or the anger stage of change, or in a job because he's the CEO's brother. Any number of circumstances may apply. The problem relates in all probability to selection and placement, not training. Management needs to consider interventions other than training. Training won't "fix" the problem.

Now consider an employee who would fit into quadrant B. This person knows the job but displays low motivation. This person may be burned out, waiting to retire, or retired in place. Often managers send subordinates of this type to training in an attempt to motivate them. Does it work? Hardly ever. The worker becomes a prisoner in the training class. The person is there "because my boss sent me." Training should not represent a punishment. Managers should use training to provide skills needed for the job. The organization, and employee, might benefit more from an opportunity for open discussion, coaching, and work system redesign.

How about the employee in quadrant C? This employee appears perfect, with high motivation and high job skills. But, how do you keep that employee? Training? No! Employees like these possess the skills to do the job. Training should not be used as a reward or time away from work.

These employees might benefit from job enrichment. They might act as mentors or buddies to new employees, work on special projects, serve on task forces, or get delegated tasks. If nothing happens, these employees won't stay on the job but will retire in place, burn out, or leave. An intervention is called for, just not training.

Quadrant D represents the only real training problem. The employee who fits in this quadrant possesses high motivation, but low job knowledge. The supervisor and the employee need to discuss the performance issues. Together, they should develop an action plan to enable the employee to gain the skills he or she needs. This action plan might include external training workshops, internal classes, professional conferences, self-directed study with guidance, or on-the-job training with a skilled co-worker.

By ferreting out training problems and applying training interventions only where needed, training project managers can substantially reduce training costs in the organization.

Training project managers need to do the following:

- accept accountability for cost containment, not for filling up training classes

- develop savvy in both business skills and in the business in which they work

- view themselves as organizational leaders with accountabilities and responsibilities linked to the business

- manage their functions through planning, directing, organizing, and controlling

- evaluate programs

- shift from measuring the number of people who attended a workshop to measuring improvements in employee performance.

Alignment of Training and Development with the Organization's Culture

Training should either fit the organization's culture or serve as one of the components in an intervention to change it. In *Corporate Culture and Performance,* Kotter and Hesket (1992) discuss the results of their research on high- and low-performing organizations. They identify alignment of structural initiatives and cultural initiatives in an organization as a major factor in producing results.

Figure 2 shows the model based on their findings. Several key points emerge from the model. Notice that the left side of the model pictures a structural path to achieve results, and the right side shows the cultural one. From the top of the model, mission guides the structural side, and vision leads the cultural one. From the mission, or structural side, come strategic objectives, which drive operational objectives, which drive activities to get results. Companies in the United States have traditionally worked this side. Management by Objectives represents a prime example of this type of principle.

From the vision, or right side, come values, practices, and behavior. Organizations in the United States have not generally focused on the culture side to achieve results. Often attempts to address the cultural side receive the reputation as "warm and fuzzy" and get dismissed.

Both structure and culture represent ways to achieve results. Kotter and Hesket found that alignment, motivation, organization, and control can help performance, but only if the resulting actions fit an intelligent business strategy for the specific environment in which a firm operates. Performance will

Figure 2. Alignment of structural and cultural initiatives for an organization's high performance.

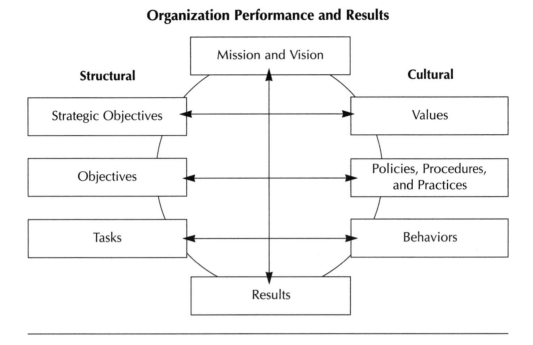

Organization Performance and Results

not be enhanced if the common behaviors and methods of doing business do not fit the needs of a firm's product or service market, financial market, and labor market. Strong cultures with practices that do not fit a company's context can actually lead intelligent people to behave in ways that are destructive—that systematically undermine an organization's ability to survive and prosper.

The database for their study included nine to 10 firms in 22 different industries in the United States. The study included 207 companies and took place between 1977 and 1989. When compared with low performers, high performers had the following results:

- revenue increase of 786 percent versus 166 percent
- workforce expansion of 282 percent versus 36 percent
- stock price increase of 901 percent versus 74 percent
- net income increase of 756 percent versus 1 percent.

11

Figure 3. Alignment of what companies do with how they do it for greatest performance.

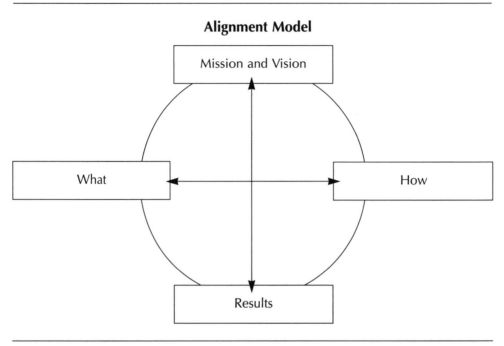

In other words, companies that match what they do with how they do it get the greatest results. Figure 3 depicts the simplified model.

If an organization wants to change its culture, management needs to state that as a strategic objective under the mission. The organization should identify and align its strategic objective with the corresponding value. This value change would affect policies, practices, and procedures.

For example, an organization might state a strategic objective: "Issue an initial public offering in three years." Its value that aligns with the strategic objective might be "We value our employees and their contribution to the business." Its practice that aligns is "Offer stock at the time of the initial offering at a reduced amount to employees." Examples of how training might support this are one-on-one sessions with financial planners, workshops on public investing, job aids for phone numbers, how to access stock prices, and how to sign up for the plan.

When there is a disconnection between the structure and values, it should be clear that there's a need for a plan for a proposed change. The change plan should incorporate appropriate organizational interventions, one of which might be training. Training would then be one of the support systems to produce the results of a change in culture. A training program alone would not change an organizational culture.

In today's transformational organizations, training functions should set just-in-time and needs-specific training as objectives. The development of training programs represents a labor-intensive activity. It takes time to design, develop, and deliver training, and the amount of time estimated scares management: 40 hours of development per instructor-led contact hour, 300 for computer-based training, and upwards of 400 for multimedia training. Line managers want training yesterday.

How can training project managers cut product cycle time? How can they manage training program development? The next chapter answers these questions.

2

Training Program Management

Rothwell and Cookson (1997) state that planning activities for training programs often occur in organizations without regard to good program planning practices or to the essential competencies needed to plan effective programs. They define program planning as a

> comprehensive process in which program planners, exercising a sense of professional responsibility, designate specific strategies to engage relevant contexts, design specific sets of learning outcomes, and plan relevant administrative aspects. (Rothwell & Cookson, 1997)

Unfortunately in many organizations, these planning activities tend to get juggled in as time permits. Moreover, training program planners may lack training or experience in project management. This results in duplication of effort as well as wasted time, work, and money. When it comes to planning training programs, the saying "I never have enough time to do it right, but always enough to do it over" all too often fits.

Do any of these scenarios sound familiar to you?

● A system, process, or policy goes into effect tomorrow. Implementation plans neglected training, and the request for expenditure did not include the training sessions in the budget. The results: No one knows how to operate the system, fill out the paperwork to initiate the process, or apply the specifications of the policy. Training should have taken place yesterday. Now, it's too late to assess needs, design, and develop the training.

● A client wanted you to tailor a time management program for his department. You held focus groups to identify needs, worked with managers to define objectives, and developed a workshop with interactive learning experiences to meet your client's requirements. The smile sheet evaluations were glowing. In order to meet your deadlines, you decided to write all of the documentation for the program at the end. After the program was completed, you moved on to another project. Now, six months later, another client wants you to develop a similar time management program for his department. Because you have no documentation, you must begin again at square one.

● As the manager of the central training and development function in a large organization, your area offers a wide program of training courses. Your department publishes the calendar of training programs and distributes them to employees within the organization. Yesterday, your manager asked you to prepare an annual report, which he will submit to the vice president of human resources. He wants you to summarize the departments that sent people to your programs, outcomes achieved, and bottom-line results your training effected. The only records you kept contain the number of people who attended your classes, the class dates, and the length of the class.

What can training program planners do to avoid these situations? How can they move from planning programs to managing projects?

ISD Program Planning Methodology Description

Instructional systems design (ISD) provides program planners with a systematic process to use when they need to develop programs. For years, ISD has provided the foundation on which training programs were built.

Chuck Hodell (1997) defines instructional systems design as a systems approach to analyzing, designing, developing, implementing, and evaluating any instructional experience. ISD is a linear process in which one stage leads to another, from analysis through evaluation, as figure 4 shows. When program planners apply ISD, they guide their project along this sequence. They complete one stage before going to the next, and once they complete a stage, they do not revisit it.

Figure 4. ISD stages and flow.

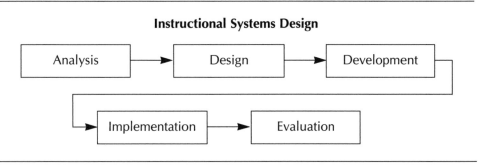

Each stage of ISD contains activities and produces outcomes. For a description of each stage, its activities, and its outcomes, see table 1.

Although ISD provides a guideline for program planners to follow, it leaves the specific activities to be carried out in each stage to the discretion of program planners. ISD offers a conceptual basis for program development, but program planners may apply ISD differently for each program they develop. The purpose of ISD is to provide a systematic approach to program development, not a tool for managing the project.

Yet the first activity in the analysis stage is often enough to turn managers against the program. Typically when they hear the term *needs assessment,* they go crazy. They say a needs assessment takes too much time, costs too much money, and involves too many people. Program planners know the value of assessing needs and what can happen to a program when it doesn't get done. But, how can they convince management of this?

To change managers' minds, training program planners need tools and processes that would enable them to manage projects, not plan programs. They need tools to transform the planning function into a process. These tools would give the training program planner credibility in managers' eyes and transform them from program planners to project managers.

Table 1. Stages, activities, and outcomes of ISD.

Stage	Description	Activities	Outcomes
Analysis	First stage of ISD, during which examination of organizational environment, prospective participants, and the performance expectations take place	Needs assessment Task analysis Job analysis	Identification of performance gaps, program goals, and audience instructional needs
Design	Defines the basic foundation and structure for the training project	Instructional objectives Instructional evaluation techniques and tasks Program evaluation plan Course sequence and structure Logic and objective maps Draft copies of materials	Design document
Development	Construction stage in which planners translate instructional strategies into instructional materials	Participant and instructor materials Support materials Computer-based materials Formative pilot testing	Manuals Media Formative evaluation Program package and delivery

Implementation	Transitional phase in which projects are placed in service	Pilot test Program delivered Evaluation by learners, facilitators, and clients Revisions	Evaluation of learners' achievement of objectives, program design, materials, and implementation plans Revisions to program based on pilot
Evaluation	Thread running through all phases	Confirmation of program appropriateness Consultation with clients Project completion Review and act on evaluations	Summative evaluation Reports on evaluation plan Project closure

Unlike program planners, project managers must find ways to cut the cycle time and offer their products in response to business needs. Moreover, project managers need flexibility and adaptability to function in today's environment of constant change.

In today's downsized organizations, project managers must manage time, resources, vendors, contractors, budgets, research and development, facilities, staff, projects, and so forth. They do not have the luxury of spreading training program development over long spans of time. Training departments have experience and continue to experience the threat of staff reductions. Over the past few years, surveys of the field have shown a substantial increase in the ratio of trainers to employees served. Because of decreased staff and increased workload, training project managers find that they must do more with less.

As a way to decrease costs and cut back to their core business, organizations have moved away from internal training and have begun hiring the training consulting firms that have become more prevalent. These firms do program planning both for their own products and in response to their clients' needs for customized programs.

Organizations that outsource want to pay one price and get a finished project. They do not want to pay their outsource provider to conduct needs assessments or other forms of research and development (R&D), and many of them don't want to do that research in-house either.

What can training project managers do to decrease expenses related to assessing needs and R&D? How can they decrease cycle time and still provide a quality product? How can they manage training program planning effectively? The next section answers these questions.

Training Program Project Management Methodology

In today's competitive environment, organizations strive to become high-performance workplaces. In *Responding to Workplace Change,* McCain and Pantazis (1997) define a high-performance workplace as an "organization that both produces and sustains competitive success through creating an environment for an empowered and effective workforce … [The high-performance workplace integrates] technology, work process and organization and human resource practices."

This integration has an impact on training, work, and learning. Organizations need to look at integrating training with work to produce both learning and results. The authors further identify a

> growing influence of "new styles of leadership," reflecting less distinction between employees and managers in terms of authority and role, and the greater importance of team leadership. HRD executives also pointed out that new models of learning that account for the way people learn—in the context of work, by interacting with others and through experience—pose a "serious challenge" to the traditional "transfer" model of learning. These emerging models provide training through self-directed and team learning and will increasingly form the building blocks of another trend: how organizations learn and how they evaluate learning. (McCain & Pantazis, 1997)

Over the years, project management has been a critical success factor in new product research, product development, engineering, and technology. It plays an increasingly key role in business today. Project management techniques offer a means by which to organize work and resources so as to do more with less. They also make it possible to align training with work to produce both learning and results.

As organizations transform to a team approach, they become more project oriented. Work groups get assigned projects to accomplish. Project management skills represent competency requirements for today's business professional. The job title *project manager* exists in many of today's organizations. Training program planners can benefit from acquiring competencies in these skills and becoming project managers.

Project Management Components

Parallels exist between project management and training program planning and development. Both share these key elements of projects:

- goal orientation

- coordination of interrelated activities

- finite time frame—a defined start and end date

- limited resources

- specified outcomes

- uniqueness.

Training program project methodology (TPPM) is a project management tool that both internal and external training program planners can use to ensure that planning and implementation follow a methodical and business-oriented path. TPPM helps training program planners reinvent themselves as training project managers. It aligns training with work to produce learning and results for project managers and any teams with which they work.

ISD serves as the foundation for the methodology for training program planning. TPPM offers flexibility in that it does not represent a linear process. Project managers follow a walkway consisting of steps. By using a variety of prepared forms, or templates, tailored to the phases of ISD, project managers effectively lead and manage training projects.

TPPM expands the five linear phases of ISD into eight steps. Although project managers follow all the steps, TPPM offers flexibility. It is not lock-step. Project managers may do several steps at one time, return to a step, do steps out of sequence, and choose the activities completed within each step related to particular projects they manage. Project managers can even work on several phases at the same time, thus decreasing the critical path, which is the least amount of time to accomplish a task. The forms help them map out the project ahead of time, determine the critical path, and work on several steps simultaneously, thus reducing product cycle time.

Table 2 shows how ISD stages correspond to the steps in TPPM. Analysis in ISD becomes present/future state analysis in TPPM. Design in ISD becomes steps 2, 3, and 4 in TPPM. These three steps represent training program design, research, and resource allocation. These are the steps involving the training program's curriculum design. During the research step, the project manager investigates off-the-shelf programs and outsourcing development in addition to the subject matter.

Table 2. Comparison of stages in ISD and TPPM.

ISD Stage	Step	Training Program Planning Methodology (TPPM)
Analysis	I	Present/Future State Analysis
Design	II	Training Program Design
	III	Training Program Research
	IV	Training Program Resource Allocation
Development	V	Training Program Instructional Design
	VI	Training Program Instructional Development
Implementation	VII	Training Program Implementation Plan
Evaluation	VIII	Training Program Evaluation

Development in ISD becomes steps 5 and 6 in TPPM. A project manager gets to these steps if during resource allocation the company decided to develop the program either internally or externally, rather than purchase an off-the-shelf program. The steps involve the training program instructional design and development. If the decision was made to outsource development, the project manager may lead the team of the external consultants or act as client to the outsource firm.

Implementation in ISD becomes training program implementation plan in TPPM. This step may include both initial rollout and ongoing administration.

Evaluation in ISD becomes training program evaluation in TPPM. The step in TPPM may involve evaluation of the rollout, summative evaluation of the program, and ongoing program monitoring.

Although TPPM uses ISD as its foundation, it has additional value as a comprehensive project management tool. Project managers as well as others in the organization can use it to lead projects, design organizational interventions, develop project team members, document process, and demonstrate project management skills. Management uses the documentation for reference and historical purposes. TPPM, moreover, captures the learning in the organization, which helps the organization build a culture of learning.

Training Program Project Management Best Practices

Project management embraces several functions, which TPPM incorporates in the forms. These best practices include

- documentation
- goal definition
- communication
- statement of outcomes
- resource identification
- cost-benefit analysis
- management commitment through cost-center manager sign off
- tracking of timelines
- identification of tasks
- assignment of responsibility
- risk management
- allocation of resources
- analysis of the scope.

The management of training program planning projects requires the skill and experience to judge not only what to do but also how much to do. Each project has unique characteristics, goals, and outcomes, and some are more complicated than others. Because of time restraints, budget considerations, or limited resources, a project manager may elect to perform some activities and not others. TPPM allows the project manager freedom to focus on those critical success factors identified for each specific project.

The forms, or templates, for TPPM provide a laundry list of potential activities. The project manager chooses those required to meet the unique program needs. Some projects require all, some a few, some most. Table 3 summarizes the activities listed on the forms for each of the TPPM steps.

Table 3. The activities for each TPPM step.

Step	Description	Tasks
1	Present/future state analysis	Definition of audience* Description of needs assessment technique Description of focus group Distribution of questionnaire/survey Description of training requirements* Identification of tasks and subtasks Learning skills matrix Assessment of future performance expectations Program plan Project budget Recommendations* Cost-center manager sign-off*
2	Design	Training program goals/outcomes Training program objectives Learning objectives Learner exit competencies* Program outline Curriculum structure Cost-center manager sign-off*
3	Research	Reference materials Courseware review Media options Description of focus group Key contacts Recommendations* Cost-center manager sign-off*
4	Resource allocation	Resource allocation* Time frame estimate* Development costs* Cost justification Benefits Cost-center manager sign-off*

*Activities required for step

Continued on page 26

Table 3. The activities for each TPPM step (continued).

Step	Description	Tasks
5	Instructional design	Course code Learning objectives* Modules Frequency Organizational range Cost Length Class size Media Hardware/software requirements Course outline*
6	Instructional development	Guidelines Instructor's manual Participant manual* Coordinator's manual Administrator's manual Collateral material Script Course description Storyboard Media development
7	Implementation plan	Implementation schedule* Pilot tests Formative evaluation Administrative procedures Roll-out strategy Measurements/outcomes* Evaluation plan Cost-center manager sign-off*
8	Program evaluation	Summary of program costs* Learner reaction sheet Summary of learning Follow-up Identification of return-on-investment Summary of implementation Summary of benefits* Cost-center manager sign-off*

*Activities required for step

TPPM provides the following:

- **Consistent process for course development.** TPPM provides a process-oriented approach for program planning. Project managers perfect the process to effect consistent results. Each time a project manager applies the process he or she develops and refines program-planning skills. The methodology allows the project manager to focus on the program and not reinvent the wheel with each new program plan.

- **Checklist for project management.** The methodology contains guidelines for the project manager to follow to manage the process. It serves as a road map for the project manager. The forms provide a structure that the project manager modifies.

- **Sign-off points for management.** Through specified sign-off points, management stays involved and linked to the process. The project manager does not own the project. The project represents a collaborative effort of the project manager and line management. This dual involvement provides a method for line management to demonstrate commitment to the project.

- **Feedback to management and clients on progress.** TPPM provides a simple, easy way to report back to management and clients on progress. The forms eliminate the need for the project manager to write and the client to read long wordy reports. The forms contain information on what was actually accomplished.

- **Documentation of work.** The forms provide a vehicle in which to keep a history of what happened as well as the decisions reached and why. They describe what worked, didn't work, and why.

- **Adherence to concepts of ISD.** TPPM provides a practical way to apply principles of ISD in a work environment.

- **Involvement of stakeholders.** Training courses affect many people. A project manager needs to get their buy-in so they support the final product. The forms give a means to identify and involve the key players from the very beginning in the training program development.

- **Consideration of learning style and media delivery differences.** TPPM provides a way to identify delivery media, address principles of adult learning, and apply techniques geared to differences in learning styles.

- **Team approach for development.** TPPM facilitates building the team and helping it to work effectively during the project. Through involving a group of people, at specified times, for different roles, the project manager builds ownership and excitement for the training. This involvement also helps with implementation.

- **Lead several projects at a time.** TPPM allows the project manager to allot time frames to steps, identify the critical path, and estimate the deadline. The forms also enable the planner to work on several steps at the same time, track, and manage them.

- **Monitor program-planning progress.** The forms provide for documentation and history of the project. They provide a reference for future program development and comparison.

- **Identify resources, timelines, and costs.** The forms provide a vehicle for estimating resources, times for each step, and costs.

- **Analyze costs, benefits, and outcomes.** By using the forms, the project manager summarizes the program costs, benefits, and outcomes.

At the outset, the project manager sets time frames with target dates and identifies which steps can proceed simultaneously. The time from start to finish becomes the critical path. Each program has its own critical path. An example of how a project manager might schedule the steps of TPPM appears in Figure 5.

Project managers derive these benefits from the methodology:

- reduced training development time
- ownership in training program from key players
- communication among units
- identification and control of the cost of course development
- definition of mastery- (competency-) level requirements
- customer involvement
- development of customer-oriented programs
- tracking of time for curriculum development
- introduction of product and training simultaneously

Figure 5. A schedule for each step of TPPM.

Training Program Planning

Training Program Planning Methodology Step	January	February	March	April	May	June	July	August	September	October
Present/Future State Analysis	■									
Training Program Design		■								
Training Program Research				■						
Training Program Resource Allocation					■					
Training Program Instructional Design						■				
Training Program Instructional Development								■		
Training Program Implementation Plan									■	
Training Program Evaluation		■								■

29

- proactive rather than reactive training
- focus of training on business needs
- definition of the benefits of training
- cost justification.

Limited Resources and TPPM

Every project manager must deal with the limited resources of personnel, time, money, and equipment. The effective project manager learns to juggle the resources available to maximize their use.

Project managers frequently establish project teams to help them juggle. Typically, project teams are made up of a large cast of characters from throughout an organization. By soliciting ideas from team members, project managers are able to use the team to gain acceptance of the project and produce a product that satisfies their organization's needs. These project teams serve a dual purpose by helping to produce a better training product and by providing a learning model for the members. As the project team assists in producing the training, it is going through the project and learning it. The team embodies the principles of integrating learning with work to produce training. Members of the team learn, the team itself learns, and the organization learns, thus emulating a learning organization. The team is modeling what it is preaching.

More often than not, members of project teams wear several hats on the team and play different roles at different times. A list of the many different roles members of a project team may play appears in table 4.

Team members join and leave the project team as needed, so adaptability and flexibility become critical skills for project managers, who often must function in a world of ambiguity. Project managers bring structure to organized chaos. They manage the project to produce desired outcomes with a fluid work team whose members come and go. Table 5 summarizes a project team's roles associated with each TPPM step.

To manage time, another limited resource, project managers set target dates, monitor progress, and follow up on assignments. Project managers are

Table 4. Project roles and responsibilities.

Role	Description
Project manager	Responsible for communicating the purpose, assigning tasks and responsibilities, setting schedules and ensuring that deadlines are met, arranging for resources, approving and controlling budgetary expenses, monitoring and evaluating progress, reporting status, releasing the product, reporting results.
Management	Assigns personnel, informs superiors of progress, prepares reports, anticipates problems, resolves conflicts, allocates resources, identifies need, plans.
Instructional designer	Designs the overall instructional model. This includes program description, instructional approach, objectives, delivery method, media, collateral material, and support systems.
Subject matter expert	Provides information about content and resources relating to all aspects of the topics for planned instruction; is responsible for checking accuracy of content treatment in activities, materials, and examinations.
Clerical, coordination, administrative support	Produces course materials, coordinate events, perform administrative duties, arrange for facilities, schedule instructors, enroll learners, coordinate programs, order supplies, set up facilities, and the like.
Clients, sponsor	Identifies the need for the project, initiates it, and owns it.
Customers	Uses the product.
Course developer	Produces written instructional materials.
Writers or scriptwriter	Writes the course and collateral materials.
Course author	Develops the interactive portions for the course.
Programmers	Uses software to write code and programs for the course.

Continued on page 32

Table 4. Project roles and responsibilities (continued).

Role	Description
Technical support	Provides technical support for equipment, software, network.
Evaluator	Person qualified to assist the project team in developing testing instruments for pretesting and for evaluating student learning (posttesting); responsible for gathering and interpreting data during program tryouts and for determining effectiveness and efficiency of the program when fully implemented.
Instructor or facilitator	Person who delivers instruction; skilled in teaching procedures and the requirements of the instructional program; with guidance from the designer, capable of carrying out details of many planning elements; responsible for trying out and then implementing the instructional plan that is developed.

responsible for bringing in the project on time and within budget. Thus, a project manager must maintain a master plan that tracks tasks, responsibilities, and due dates for each step in TPPM.

Project managers confront numerous challenges that can affect time. Often some employees get short-term assignments on the team, and these people have differing sets of priorities. Project teams may also depend on people outside the team—both within and outside of the organization—for a variety of tasks. All too often, people do not perform their tasks on time, causing a projected target date to slip. Because project tasks frequently follow a sequence, when one date is missed it creates a domino effect, causing other project tasks in the sequence to be late. The delay in one task can hold up the entire project, jeopardizing the "drop dead" date for delivery of the project. Project managers who deal with the challenge of delivering a project on time must have problem-resolution skills.

Project managers must also deal with constraints of money and equipment. Unexpected costs, budget cuts, or unrealistic budget projections affect a project manager's ability to turn out a product on time and within budget.

Table 5. Project team roles for each TPPM step.

Step	TPPM	Potential Roles
1	Present/future state analysis	Program planner Clerical support Client Customers Management Researcher Needs analyst Program designer
2	Training program design	Program planner Instructional designer Clerical support Course developer Subject matter expert Client Management Program designer Researcher Instructor and facilitator Learning specialist
3	Training program research	Program planner Instructional designer Clerical support Course developer Subject matter expert Client Customers Management Learning specialist Researcher Instructor or facilitator Evaluator
4	Training program resource allocation	Program planner Client Management
5	Training program instructional design	Program planner Clerical support Instructional designer Course developer Subject matter expert Instructor or facilitator Scriptwriter/writer Course author Coordination support

Continued on page 34

Table 5. Project team roles for each TPPM step (continued).

Step	TPPM	Potential Roles
5 (cont'd)	Training program instructional design (cont'd)	Technical support Programmer Client Customer Management Learning specialist
6	Training program instructional development	Program planner Clerical support Instructional designer Course developer Subject matter expert Instructor or facilitator Scriptwriter or writer Course author Programmer Technical support Coordination support Client Customer Learning specialist
7	Training program implementation plan	Program planner Instructional designer Course developer Subject matter expert Instructor or facilitator Clerical support Coordination support Technical support Administrative support Client Customer Management Marketer
8	Training program evaluation	Program planner Clerical support Instructional designer Course developer Course facilitator Coordination support Administrative support Client Customer Management Evaluator

Equipment availability, various contentious issues—over equipment, budgets, and the like—or limitations in other areas may have an impact on the budget as well as on project outcomes.

The ability to determine and decide when the project is complete represents a critical success factor for project managers. The effective project manager can answer these questions related to each unique project: How good is good enough? What is complete? Do we go for 100 percent or compromise with 80 percent? What is the cost involved? What value does it add? Is the incremental expense worth it?

Project managers' jobs are easier if they have organizational techniques, processes, and tools. The steps in TPPM provide a path or process for the project manager and organizational techniques to help them track and manage the project. By tailoring the forms, project managers can fit them to each unique project.

A Guide to TPPM

The chapters that follow are a guide to the use of TPPM. Each chapter covers one step. It puts the step into context, explains the elements of the form, provides instructions in use of the form, and describes the necessary resources project managers and teams will use. Case studies in chapters 3, 5, 6, 7, and 9 put the forms into context by showing how they've been used. Chapter 4 provides a sample of a completed form for step 2.

3

Step 1:
Present/Future State
Analysis

Training usually takes place in an organization because someone identifies a performance gap; a business problem that needs to be resolved; a new product, equipment, or service; a business need; or a change in the way people will work. The person decides that training is the best way to fill the gap, resolve the problem, or introduce the change. That person often becomes the client or sponsor of the training product.

A project manager is necessary as the program begins to take shape. The first step, present/future state analysis, takes time because it involves the preliminary work. In this step, the project manager defines the problem and either shapes the program or identifies other approaches. Training doesn't always represent the best way to handle every situation. Methods that might be more appropriate in other situations include other job aids, work flow changes, or work redesign. If training is not the best approach, the project ends at this step.

The job aid for this step, the present/future state analysis form, appears in figure 6.

Often one or two people can complete most or all of the activities in this step, so it may not yet be necessary to create a project team. If the project continues beyond step 1, it will be necessary to name members of the team and define their commitment.

Figure 6. Present/future state analysis form.

Project Team: _____

    _____

    _____

Audience:
(Describe the population that the training intervention addresses.)

Description of Needs Assessment:
(Describe the method used for identifying training requirements (that is, job task analysis, questionnaire, benchmark other organizations, survey, interview, job/performance/skill gaps, needs assessment. Attach copies of documents used.)

Focus Group Members:
(Describe the customers who participated in focus groups.)

Questionnaires and Surveys:
(Describe any questionnaires, surveys, or other instruments used to assess training requirements.)

Identification of Tasks and Subtasks:
(List activities related to on-the-job performance. Identify major tasks or applications, or both, by target audience.)

Learning Skills Matrix:
(Attach a copy of a skill matrix related to the tasks or applications, or to both.)

Assessment of Future Performance Expectations:
(Describe the process used to define the goals for the future.)

Focus Group Members:
(Describe the customers who participated in focus groups for the assessment of future performance expectations.)

Training Requirements:
(Identify specific training requirements.)

Training Program Plan:
(Describe the time frames for each step and create a Gantt chart to depict the time frames and overlapping of steps.)

Recommendations:
(State recommendation for interventions to meet identified performance requirements.)

Cost-Center Manager: _____Date: _____

Depending on the situation, the project manager may complete all of the activities in the step, may complete only some of them, or may add other activities. Each form provides a list of possibilities from which the project manager can add or delete. Project managers should tailor the forms to their applications, situations, clients, and time frames. The forms represent job aids, not cement. They provide guidelines to follow, which the project manager customizes as needed.

Communicating With Key Players

At the beginning and end of this step, it's generally good practice to hold a meeting of key players. Key players might include the project's sponsor, your supervisor, the client's supervisor, representatives from the target audience, project team or potential members, potential resources to the project team, outside consultants, and staff from the human resources department. During the initial meeting, discuss program goals, parameters, expected outcomes, roles, responsibilities, accountabilities, and timelines.

At the end of the step, send them a copy of the completed form with a cover memo requesting a meeting. The key people or project team, if there is one, should then meet with the sponsor to discuss the project's progress to date, current status, and the action plan. The project manager should be careful to keep to the agenda. Adherence to principles of good meeting practices shows sensitivity to people's time, organizational skills, and project leadership. At the end of the meeting, get management's sign off. Follow this process for each step that requires management to sign off. For step 1, if training is not the best approach, the meeting will provide closure for the project.

Completing the Form

Project team: Each form begins with places for listing the members of the project team. Because the project manager may not yet have a team, the lines may remain blank for step 1.

Project managers who have a team may choose to list only the names of the members of the team, or they may want to include such additional information as each member's title, department, location, and business unit, or that a team member is a consultant. Consistency is a key. If project managers list only the people's names on this form, they should only put names on all the other forms.

It's important to list everyone who participated as a member of the project team during this stage. Only active project team members belong on the list, not people who served as resources, subject matter experts, or members of focus groups. Because the project team's membership may vary during the project, it's important to document who was involved during the various stages.

Audience: This section refers to the group of people for whom the training is intended. The audience might be, for example, sales support staff, the accounting department, or all employees with less than six months' service. A list of names doesn't belong here, just a description of the group. It is important to complete this section for every project.

Description of needs assessment: The processes, procedures, or techniques the project manager used to identify the need for training belong here. Although the completion of this section is optional, it represents a critical component in the training program design and is recommended.

Depending on the type of program, time restraints, and staff limitations, project managers might assess training needs by conducting a survey, sending out a questionnaire, interviewing people, researching literature, discussing options with a vendor, observing people at work, talking to representatives in other organizations, and the like. Describe the process as fully as you can. Include the rationale for doing what you did, reasons for selecting the population, restrictions, and conclusions. Literature supports the use of both expert performers and low performers for needs assessment purposes. By comparing the results of a high performer with those of a low performer, you can more easily identify what separates the two categories of worker.

Write the description clearly enough that you could replicate the process if you needed to. Remember that today what you are doing is foremost in your mind, makes perfect sense, and seems like the only way, but three years from now you may not remember what you did. So, write the description as if you were going to read it three years from now.

When conducting the needs assessment, project managers should consider technology for speed of delivery and ease in data compilation, computation, and analysis. E-mail, the Internet, or a company's intranet access can be effective ways to communicate questionnaires or surveys.

If you do not complete this section, make sure you include the concepts under one of the other sections.

Focus group members: Focus groups represent one of the options for needs assessment. If you choose to hold focus groups to determine needs, list the people who participate. Literature validates selecting both champions and protagonists for focus groups. Again you may list only their names, or you may wish to include titles, location, department, business unit, and other types of identification.

The project team may wish to conduct the focus group by audio or video conferencing. If the focus group uses electronic means, your description should include some of the following information: contacts, costs, benefits, procedures, contracts, resources needed, materials produced, processes, and communication methods.

Complete this section only if you use a focus group.

Questionnaires and surveys: If you choose to distribute questionnaires or conduct surveys to assess training needs, describe them here. Include examples of communications, return rates, compilation of data, analysis, conclusions, and the like. The more thorough you are in your documentation, the more use the forms will be to you.

Generally questionnaires used for needs assessment seek to identify the criticality of the skill for the job and the level of proficiency needed. Sometimes, assessment includes frequency. Many needs assessors use Likert scales as anchors for answers to questionnaire statements. By doing this, they can compile data more easily. Figure 7 shows a portion of a typical needs assessment questionnaire.

Complete this section only if you use questionnaires or surveys.

Identification of tasks and subtasks: Often referred to as a job or task analysis, this listing is one of the techniques to assess training needs. To complete this assessment, you may wish to observe workers on the job and record

Figure 7. Sample needs assessment questionnaire.

Skill Area	Importance	Ability
Effectively guide and direct performance by providing meaningful feedback with an emphasis on employee growth and development		
Ability to effectively assign work tasks and assignments according to direct reports' proficiency for successfully completing them		

their activities, or you may wish to ask workers to complete forms or logs. Either method tends to be labor intensive, generate much data, and present difficulty compiling. This section is optional.

Learning skills matrix: This matrix correlates job skills and required proficiency levels. It is a tool the project team and later the supervisors can use to identify training needs, define expectations, or structure classes. Figure 8 shows a typical learning skills matrix in an Information Systems Department.

This section is optional.

Figure 8. Learning skills matrix in an information systems department.

Skill Area	Programmer	Programmer or Analyst	Senior Programmer or Analyst	Project Leader
Uses e-mail	A	C	C	P
Uses voice-mail system	C	C	C	C
Uses word-processing software	A	C	C	P
Uses spreadsheet software	A	C	C	P

N = not needed on the job; A = aware (should know about skill); C = competent (able to use skill on job); P = proficient (able to perform at an advanced level)

Assessment of future performance expectations: Use this section to describe how you determined future performance expectations. This section is particularly valuable when you are designing training for new equipment, systems, processes, and the like. Organizations frequently use techniques like the following to define future performance expectations: interviews with vendors of new equipment, benchmarking other organizations, alignment with strategic objectives, and literature searches. This section is optional.

Training requirements: This section contains a statement of the training requirements based on an analysis of the needs assessment. The more specifically and succinctly you state the requirements, the better. These requirements serve to drive the remainder of the project. If they are faulty, you will have difficulty throughout the project. If the requirements are clear up-front, the project will tend to progress more smoothly. This section is required.

Training program plan: In this section, you describe your action plan for the project. Although it may change, and probably will, think out carefully your plan of attack for the project. The more detailed, thorough, complete, and realistic you are at this early stage, the more probable is the success of your project. Gantt charts can help to identify critical paths and give a projected completion date. They also provide visual clues to where steps might overlap, bottleneck, and create contingencies. Although this section is optional, you will probably find you need to complete it most of the time.

Project budget: In this section, itemize the costs and benefits to the training. Estimate as closely as possible the development costs. The more exact you are at this point, the easier it will be later on. This section is optional.

Recommendations: This section contains your project team's recommendations. It should detail the interventions you suggest to meet performance expectations. Although you may choose to describe only the intervention or interventions that have been selected, there are advantages to describing all the interventions the project team considered. A listing of the other options provides the team with documentation, later reference, closure, elimination of rework to research other options suggested by management, and completeness.

Cost-center manager's signature: The last line in the form calls for a cost-center manager's signature and date. That manager should be the sponsor. If the sponsor and the person whose budget the project comes out of are different, get both people to sign the form. By requesting the sponsor's signature, the project manager keeps that person involved, helps to create a business partnership, and facilitates communication.

Resources

The necessary resources for this step are as follows:

● **People:** The minimum roles are the project manager, the client, and clerical support.

● **Time:** The time to complete the step depends on the type of assessment instruments chosen, such as questionnaires and surveys, focus groups, secondary sources, and observation. Respondents typically get 10 working days to complete questionnaires and surveys. Problems with timing may occur if response rates are low, and it becomes necessary to follow up. Focus groups have the advantage of providing data at one time, but they require up-front coordination. Reviews of secondary sources such as performance records and historical training needs are a less time-intensive option. Observation requires two people and may not include a representative sampling unless taken over a period of time.

● **Cost:** Costs may include people's time, mailing, printing, access fees for conferencing, incentives for questionnaires, travel, and other activities.

● **Equipment:** This step may require a variety of equipment including office-automation software, such as word processing, spreadsheets, and databases. Project management software can provide project managers with assistance in planning. This type of tool assists in the generation of Gantt charts, defining time frames, identifying the critical path, and setting goals and outcomes for each phase.

Step 1 Case Study:
Training Needs Assessment

During their annual objective-setting meeting, the corporate Organizational Development and Training Department (OD&T) in a large chemical and drug manufacturer identified a business challenge. The department experienced increasing numbers of no-shows for courses, last-minute cancellations, and decreases in the ratings of courses on learner reaction sheets. This led to duplication of work, wasted effort, and decreased customer satisfaction.

Department members identified a disconnect among courses offered, internal customers' training requirements, and actual demand, and they also noted that the course locations were too far for many of the employees. The department set as a strategy to move from an activity-based focus to an impact-based one. Because their audience consisted of supervisors and managers throughout the organization, the department conducted a corporate-wide needs assessment. Goals set for the needs assessment included the following:

- identifying the highest training needs
- matching the training needs to skills provided within courses
- prioritizing the delivery of classes
- matching training with employee developmental needs.

The department partnered with the task force that had developed the Corporate Performance Management System. This system defined the categories and skills that professionals within the organization needed.

Members of OD&T identified learning outcomes for courses related to the critical job skills identified on the performance management system. The department developed a self-assessment instrument listing skill requirements from the performance management system. Employees used a five-point Likert scale to rank the importance of the skill to their job along with their individual competency. To ensure that responses were anonymous, an outside consulting agency compiled the information.

The analysis of the data provided a numerical listing of the skills. This listing enabled the department to identify courses that addressed the needed skills. If no course existed, the department used TPPM to develop them.

4

Step 2:
Program Design

Step 2 initiates training program planning using the recommendations agreed to in the current/future state analysis form. This step corresponds to curriculum design.

TPPM differentiates between curriculum and instructional design. In TPPM, curriculum design refers to the subject matter content, practices, and exit competencies that make up the whole program. You might, therefore, think of curriculum design as an educational umbrella covering many topics. These topics, in turn, may become individual modules, sessions, or classes. Curriculum design in step 2 takes a helicopter view of the content. During this step, the project team approaches the project holistically by viewing the entire, finished puzzle, and then it works to break it into individual pieces.

Instructional design gets into the pieces of puzzle. When the project team does the instructional design in step 5, it defines individual classes, identifies instructional strategies, and manages the instructional process. In step 5, the project team completes the actual instructional design, development, and materials for the program.

In this step, however, during the curriculum design process, the project team considers training as a whole and then breaks it into manageable pieces. Team members must define their mission, and strategic goals and then cascade program goals, outcomes, objectives, and competencies, with one falling out of the other.

Following Kotter and Hesket's (1992) corporate culture and performance model, the project manager needs to ensure that the course design aligns both strategically and culturally with the organization for the best results to occur. The form in figure 9 provides a guide to help the project manager move through this step.

Completing the Form

Project team: Use the same format on this form as you did on the one for step 1. Because different people may participate as members of the project team at different times during this step, make sure you list everyone. Keep in mind that they may only appear as a member of the project team on this form. For consistency, historical purposes, and team building, strive to keep a core membership of key people.

Figure 9. Training program design form.

Project Team: _____

_____

_____

Training Program Outcomes and Goals:
(Describe the goals of the overall program in measurable terms.)

Training Program Objectives:
(Describe overall training program objectives.)

Participant Exit Competencies:
(Describe in measurable terms the performance levels that participants will achieve.)

Learning Objectives:
(Describe in behavioral terms the learning objectives and competency levels for interventions in the program. Identify specific courses, sequences, prerequisites, and standards of measurement for successful demonstration of competency.)

Program Outline:
(Define the topics and subjects to include in the program.)

Curriculum Structure:
(Illustrate the curriculum sequence for the overall program.)

Cost-Center Manager: _____Date: _____

Training program outcomes and goals: The project manager and the team must define the program outcomes in measurable terms that provide a way to evaluate the success of the training program. What will the organization gain through the program? The outcomes that answer this question should be hard dollar or quantifiable benefits, unlike the training program vision or goals, which are more soft dollar or qualitative benefits.

Use this section to describe anticipated outcomes and goals, or both. Many project teams state their charter or team mission in this section as well as the project outcomes.

Literature and personal experience testify to the importance of team missions. They tend to create team synergy and give direction for the team to follow in its journey. If used this way, the section parallels the mission and vision element of the Kotter and Hesket (1992) model. Program outcomes equate to the mission and the project charter to the vision. Think of a lighthouse and a ship as an analogy. The project charter represents the lighthouse, and the program outcomes represent the ship. With the charter in front, everyone on the team knows where to steer.

Training program objectives: This section describes in measurable terms what the project team anticipates achieving through the training. The purpose of the training—what it will accomplish—goes here. You can describe the purpose in quantitative or qualitative measurements, or both. This section is comparable to the strategic objectives and values element in the Kotter and Hesket (1992) model. The quantitative objectives are comparable to the strategic objectives on the structural side, and the qualitative objectives are comparable to values on the cultural side.

Project teams may choose to include both quantitative and qualitative objectives or just one. Although neither is technically required, the project team should at the very least go through an exercise to determine the added value the training provides to the organization.

Participant exit competencies: The project team must next determine what the participants will do after they finish the program, in other words, the exit competencies. The project team needs to base these exit competencies on the business requirements identified through the current/future state analysis. The project team should state these exit competencies in the form of the skills, knowledge, or abilities the participants will demonstrate or achieve through the training. At this point, the project team should not think about classes, it should focus on more generalized knowledge, attitudes, and skills. The project team should make sure that it states the exit competencies in measurable terms.

The project team should, moreover, consider exit competencies that affect both the structural and cultural sides. Using Kotter and Hesket's model, this component would relate to operational objectives and practices. For example, an exit competency for a leadership program that addresses the structural side might state: Appraise the seven principles of effective evaluation as they apply to our employee performance management process.

An example of an exit competency for the same program that addresses the cultural side might state: Develop a code of behavior when conducting employee performance appraisals consistent with the seven principles of effective evaluation.

Information contained in this section represents one of the critical success factors for the project. If the project team does not define what participants will accomplish, no one will know if they accomplished it. Or, as the Cheshire cat stated in *Alice's Adventures in Wonderland,* if you don't know where you want to go, any path will do. TPPM, therefore, requires the project team to complete this section.

Learning objectives: Learning objectives go hand in hand with exit competencies because they enable the exit competencies. They differ in the level or degree of specificity. Exit competencies represent outcomes or skills at a terminal or completed point, whereas learning objectives may represent subsequent skills, class learnings, or prerequisite abilities. The project team should state these learning objectives in behavioral terms. For example, the participant will use the annual performance review form to conduct a performance review for each employee who reports to him or her. Because learning objectives enable exit competencies, the number of learning objectives may be greater than the number of exit competencies. Performance criteria cascade from the stated learning objectives. To develop effective training, therefore, the project team needs to ensure that performance criteria do not represent higher skill level than stated in the learning objectives.

The project team needs to communicate with the sponsor and stakeholders about performance expectations. Figure 10 depicts an instructional design model for project managers as they progress through TPPM.

Figure 10. Instructional design model for TPPM.

Instructional Design Model

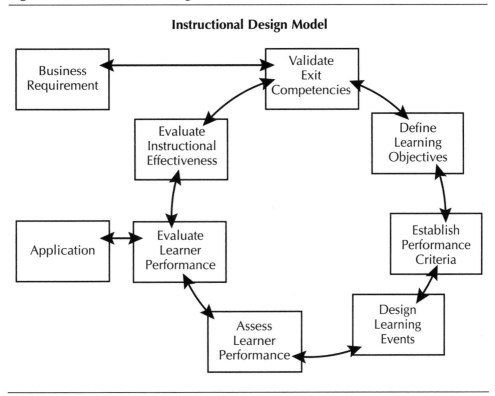

The model depicts instructional design as a loop with each element providing inputs and outputs to the others. Business requirements are an entry point into the loop and validate the exit competencies. Learning objectives get defined on the basis of the exit competencies. Next comes the establishment of the performance criteria as defined through the learning objectives, followed by design of learning events. Participant performance gets assessed through the learning events. Once performance assessments take place, learners are evaluated and apply the skills on the job. Application of skills on the job represents the participant's exit point from the loop. The evaluation of the effectiveness of the instruction is based on the evaluation of the learners' attainment of the exit competencies. Thus exit competencies get validated through instructional effectiveness as well as business requirements. These joint elements complete the loop and keep it dynamic. The model adapts as learners apply skills learned and identified business requirements change.

In TPPM, curriculum design goes to the point of identifying performance criteria; instructional design then takes over. After identification of performance criteria, the project team determines whether it will take one or many sessions to deliver them. TPPM curriculum design includes categorizing and breaking the performance criteria down into logical pieces or information chunks.

During step 2 of curriculum design, the team determines the number of sessions, their content, and the sequence. The next element of the instructional design model initiates the instructional design that TPPM covers in step 5.

Program outline: This section describes the content the project team determined for the program in the present/future state analysis. The outline should contain the content for the whole program. In the outline, the project team breaks the program down into manageable pieces—chunks of information that can be effectively grouped and delivered together.

Don't worry about the sequence of topic points or concentrate on including too much detail at this point. The outline will change. The purpose of the outline is to give the big picture in terms of content, not instruction. When the project team begins to design learning events in step 5, the sequences and order will change depending on information chunking. Although this section is not required, it can be quite helpful later on because it provides conceptually where the team is going.

Curriculum structure: Use this section to graphically or verbally represent the sequence for the program if more than one session is needed. The project team must determine entering behavior, skills learned or reinforced on the job, the performance expectations, and then any performance gaps. At this point, the team should imagine the ideal program, which may consist of one session or many sessions.

More and more organizations require just-in-time and just-what's-needed training. Rather than sending people to training programs for five days at a time, they choose shorter sessions delivered in modular form that focus on specific needs. Use this section to depict those modules, their sequence, and flow. If modules require prerequisites or job experience, state it here.

The team agrees on the scope and extent of the modules that make up the program. Quite often training alone doesn't respond to the need. Perhaps the ideal scenario calls for integrating training with the job, for example, in a point-of-use training program that incorporates performance technology and enables employees to access training when they need it. Or maybe the ideal situation makes use of distributed, or distance, learning. In this type of environment, either time or space separates the learner and instructor, by video or satellite.

Although the team considers these possibilities at this time, it will not work on the specifics until step 5. By documenting the team's thoughts, the concepts do not get lost or forgotten.

Whatever the ideal scenario, the project team should limit the scope of a class to an information chunk or piece that an employee can master and then set mastery levels and final outcomes. Where appropriate, the team should identify performance criteria. These performance criteria often are used later in step 5 as a pre- or posttest for the learner. Performance criteria also serve as an effective measurement for the success of the training.

This section is not required but presents a valuable exercise for the project team because it gets the members thinking holistically. Moreover, the visual representation through the graphing helps people see the overall project more clearly.

Cost-center manager: This form requires the cost-center manager's signature of approval. If the client is different from the person paying the bill, both should be involved. This form can become part of the client contract. The documentation contained here is critical, especially in the event that changes are made in the client contracts.

Figure 11 is an example of a completed training program design form.

Resources

The necessary resources for this step are as follows:

● **People:** The minimum roles for this step include a project manager; instructional designer; clerical, administrative, or coordination support; a subject matter expert; the client, and management.

Figure 11. Completed training program design form.

Project Team: Diana Shriver
                        Bobbi Spivak
                        Patty Jennings
                        Dale Marrison

Training Program Outcomes and Goals:
(Describe the goals of the overall program in measurable terms.)
Committees will
  • conduct effective meetings
  • use tools for problem solving and decision making
  • take and distribute minutes of meetings
  • get results.

Training Program Objectives:
(Describe overall training program objectives.)
Participants will
  • use committee tools to improve the effectiveness of meetings
  • develop an agenda for a committee meeting
  • designate roles for a committee meeting
  • conduct a committee meeting
  • record minutes for the committee meeting
  • define action items and assign responsibility
  • critique the meeting.

Participant Exit Competencies:
(Describe in measurable terms the performance levels that participants will achieve.)
Participants will
  • participate actively on committees
  • develop a charter for committees
  • apply tools to conduct effective committee meetings
  • meet regularly as a committee
  • take and distribute minutes
  • report on results.

Learning Objectives:
(Describe in behavioral terms the learning objectives and competency levels for interventions in the program. Identify specific courses, sequences, prerequisites, and standards of measurement for successful demonstration of competency.)

Learning Objective	Competency Level	Course	Measurement
Use committee tools to improve the effectiveness of meetings	Proficient	Meetings Soup to Nuts	Informal workshop assessment, observe in a meeting
Develop an agenda for a committee meeting	Competent	Meetings Soup to Nuts	Informal workshop assessment, observe in a meeting, supplemental committee documents

Continued on page 55

Figure 11. Completed training program design form (continued).

Learning Objective	Competency Level	Course	Measurement
Designate roles for a committee meeting	Confident	Meetings Soup to Nuts	Informal workshop assessment, observe in a meeting
Conduct a committee meeting	Confident	Meetings Soup to Nuts	Informal workshop assessment, observe in a meeting
Record minutes for the committee meeting	Competent	Meetings Soup to Nuts	Informal workshop assessment, recorded committee minutes
Define action items and assign responsibility	Confident	Meetings Soup to Nuts	Informal workshop assessment, supplemental committee documents
Critique the meeting	Confident	Meetings Soup to Nuts	Informal workshop assessment, observe in a meeting

Program Outline:
(Define the topics and subjects to include in the program.)

    I.   Introduction
         A. Opening
            1. Welcome
            2. Icebreaker
            3. Workshop agenda
            4. Participant handout
         B. Overview
            1. Objectives
            2. Expectations
   II. Team Process
         A. Tools and agreements
            1. Brainstorming
            2. Team agreements
            3. Consensus building
         B. Activity
  III. Effective Meetings
         A. Characteristics
         B. Purposes
            1. Share information
            2. Receive information

Continued on page 56

Figure 11. Completed training program design form (continued).

       3. Analyze and problem solve
       4. Reach group decision
       5. Generate new system or product ideas
       6. Make a recommendation and solicit feedback
       7. Explain and gain support for decision
    C. Planning
       1. Objectives
       2. Participants
       3. Agenda
       4. Logistics
       5. Audiovisual
    D. Conducting
       1. Opening
       2. During
         a. Leader's role
         b. Team roles
         c. Participation
         d. Recording
         e. Closing
         f. Follow-up
         g. Evaluating
 IV. Task Selection Tools
    A. Weighted voting
    B. Impact and trend ranking
 V. Mock Committee Meeting
 VI. Wrap-up

Curriculum Structure:
(Illustrate the curriculum sequence for the overall program.)

    Meetings Soup to Nuts
    Committee meetings follow-up

Cost-Center Manager: _____ Dorothea Bovina _____ Date: _____ 10/20/97 _____

- **Time:** The time required to complete this step depends on the complexity of the training intervention, the clarity of the recommendations from the first form, and project team members' dedication to the project. The training program design form covers a labor-intensive activity, and, therefore, time estimates need to take into consideration both how much time participants can allocate to it and whether they are committed to doing it.

- **Cost:** Costs involved in this step are associated primarily with people's time.

- **Equipment:** This step may require office automation software, including word processing, graphics, spreadsheets, and databases.

5

Step 3: Research

The next step centers on research. The curriculum design step generated the big picture of the project on the basis of inputs from the current/future state analysis. Although research took place during the first two steps, it primarily addressed problem identification. The team now undertakes research that is more focused and directed toward the solution of the problem.

During step 3, the project team identifies references and resources for the project. The references the team looks at include both those the project team will use and those customers could use for training, reinforcement, and refresher training. The project team identifies reference materials, off-the-shelf courseware, manuals, training for the project team, other organizations' approaches, and key resources.

During this time, the team begins to investigate whether it will build or buy a training program. This decision involves questions such as

- What will meet the training needs?
- What is the most cost-effective approach?
- Do we have the resources to dedicate to the project?
- Should we outsource development?
- Do training programs exist that meet our needs?

Figure 12 shows a flowchart, or decision map, to guide project managers and teams through the questions of whether to build or buy a training program as well as those on choosing an outside provider. All too often a team chooses a vendor because of a personal contact—someone knows someone. In this critical stage, the project team needs to be objective and unbiased.

The flowchart is an aid in the decision-making process. It helps identify questions for the team to ask in order to select the right vendor to develop the program. The flowchart, therefore, serves as a tool for team building.

The form to use with step 3, training program research, appears in figure 13. Team members list the different tools they consider in their research. The form lets them tailor the type of information they provide depending on the nature of the project. Through the activities done in this step, the project team builds a shared vision, learns as a team, and develops personal mastery.

Before designing and developing the project, the team must get up to speed on the project content, scope, complexity, and materials in the course. That happens here. A level setting takes place during this step, with team members enhancing their levels of confidence and competency on the project's content, scope, and complexity. The project manager may find it critical to reach down a layer and involve potential customers of the program as well as the client. By involving these customers, the project manager builds partnerships that will facilitate implementation, decrease the organizational learning curve, and develop joint ownership in the project.

Completing the Form

Project team: As usual, the names of the people participating in the project team go here. This list should include only actual identified members of the team. People who participate as resources or as a subcommittee get listed under focus group.

Reference materials: The project team uses this section to identify the resources they reviewed. These resources include books, periodicals, Web sites, online courses, training manuals, conferences, workshops, and the like. The chart in this section enables the team to summarize information for easy reference. Through documenting all of the sources, the team has a place to go

Figure 12. A decision map to building or buying a training program.

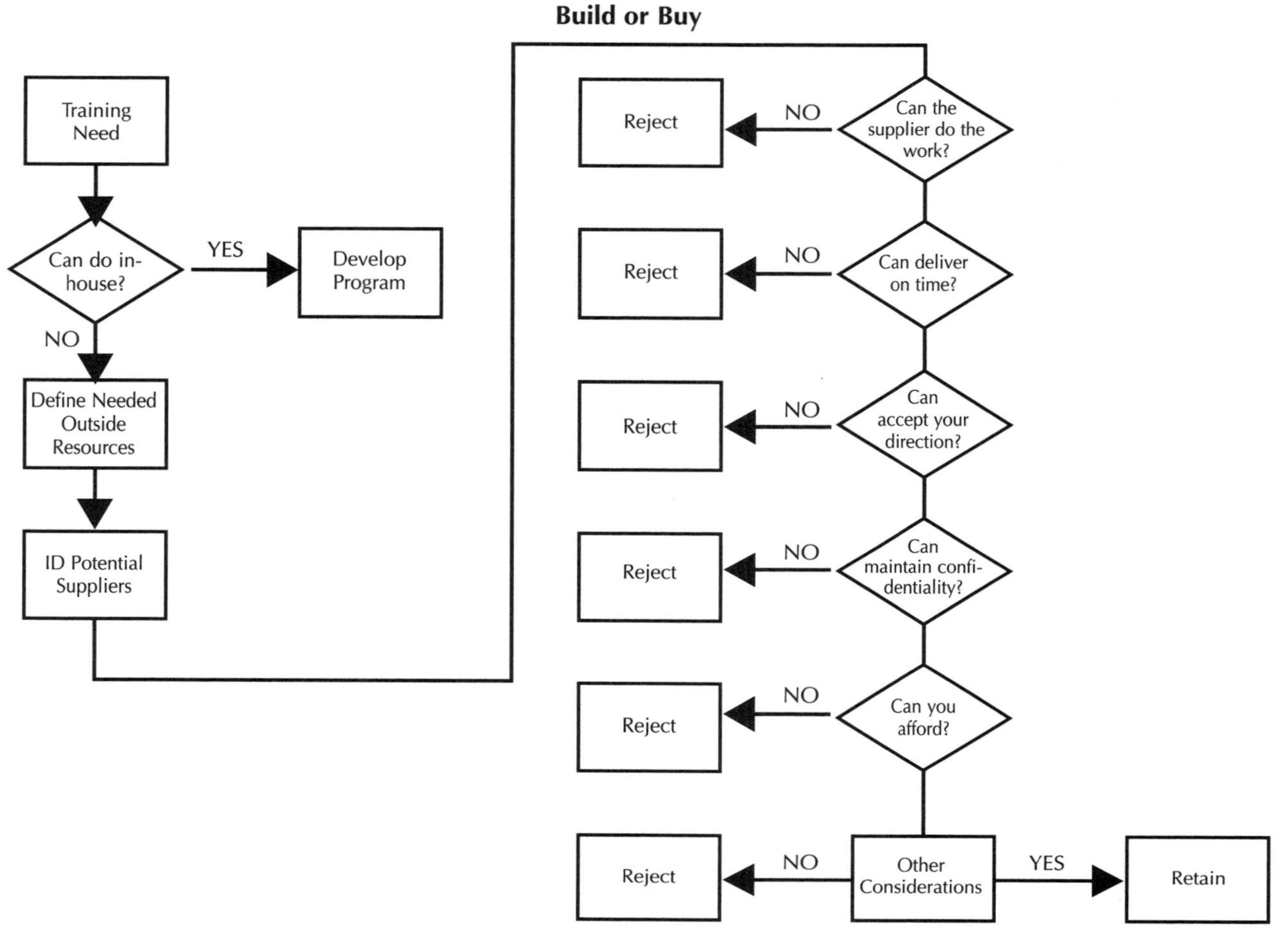

Figure 13. Training program research form.

Project Team: _____

_____

_____

Reference Materials
(List recommended references, resources, and courseware available for research, informa-
tion, and training on course content. Indicate the title, type of material (text, training
material, manual, and the like); description (what type of information is contained in the
material); provider's name and address; order number; and lead time required.)

Title	Type	Description	Provider's Name and Address	Order	Lead Time

Courseware Review:
(State process used to review off-the-shelf courseware. Identify criteria used.)

Focus Group:
(Describe the customers who participated in the focus group.)

Media Options:
(List media reviewed for training. State criteria for recommendation.)

Key Contacts:
(Within company)

(External)

Recommendation:
(Identify options and state recommendations for providing training to meet requirements.)

Cost-Center Manager: _____Date: _____

to find the answers to questions that may arise later about whether or not members looked at a particular book, read an article, or attended a workshop given by a leading guru. This section also provides a place to store information on how to order materials, where to purchase them, and how long it takes to get them. The team should not hesitate to modify the chart to fit members' needs. For example, by adding a column for costs, the team could use the form for budget purposes. An example of a completed chart appears in figure 14.

Figure 14. Example of a completed reference material chart.

Title	Type	Description	Provider's Name and Address	Order No.	Lead Time	Cost
Coaching and Feedback	Info-line	Practitioner's guide and practical tips on coaching and giving feedback to employees	ASTD Services Center Box 1567 Merrifield, VA 22116-1523 1.800.628.2783	9006	2 wks	$10 + shipping
Leadership Excellence	Work-shop	7 days Middle and Upper man-agers Focus on building high-performance teams	NTL 1240 North Pitt Street Suite 100 Alexandria, VA 22314-1403 1.800.777.5227		5 wks	$1,395
Analyzing Performance Problems	Book	Step-by-step approach to identifying and solving performance problems	Center for Effective Performance, Inc. P.O. Box 102462 Atlanta GA 30368-2462 1.800.558.3237	434	7 days	$19.95 + shipping

Figure 15. Sample courseware review form.

Criteria	Training Program 1	Training Program 2	Training Program 3
Adult Learning			
Learner centered			
Learner input into objectives			
Learning environment appropriate			
Quality of Instruction			
Defines objectives clearly			
Presents material at appropriate level			
Training useful in a work situation			
Training adequate for learners to begin using on the job			
Sessions supported with exercises related to work environment			
Exercises enable learners to apply concepts on the job			
Provides for reinforcement of learning			
Covers objectives			
Instructional Techniques			
States directions and instructions clearly			
Allows learners to progress at their own rate			
Information presented in a logical sequence			
Information presented at an appropriate pace			
Ease of Use			
Branching available			
Learners able to specify objectives			
Can end program before completion			
May take topics out of sequence			
Provides help line or other support			

Courseware review: Quite often, project teams will find off-the-shelf courseware that appears to meet its requirements. Before selecting it, however, the team should review and evaluate the courseware. Groups should set criteria and create forms to use for review to ensure that the members are comparing the same things. Figure 15 contains a sample of a courseware review form.

The project team should tailor this tool for its unique project. The figure merely represents a sample in which a team compared three programs. To rank each program, a team can use high, medium, and low; a Likert scale; plus and minus; or something else. Each team can choose its own scale, but the key is that members compare apples to apples, reach consensus on what the criteria represent, and document its system.

The team may find it helpful to include other people from the organization in the evaluation. One way to involve potential customers is through a focus group of internal and external customers. That group could, for example, provide a useful service in reviewing off-the-shelf courseware. By forming and using a focus group, the project team gains its members' input, promotes ownership in the solution and commitment, and gets recommendations. One word of caution: Project managers should stress that the team will use the focus group's comments as input into the recommendations, not decisions. It is logistically impossible to use everyone's suggestions.

Following the focus group's analysis, the project manager should attach the group members' sheets to the training program research form for a comprehensive historical record. This step can become a de facto go or no-go point for courseware development. To help reach a consensus, the project team could use the flowchart in figure 12 by substituting the word *courseware* for *supplier*. If an off-the-shelf solution fits, the team may decide to use it and not create its own program. With a decision to purchase an off-the-shelf program, the critical path for program development often decreases substantially.

Focus group: Details on a focus group the project team used—whether to critique reference materials, evaluate courseware, provide insight, or in some other way—go in this section. As with the names of the project members, the team may choose to include such pieces of information as department, location, phone number, position, and the like. The team should also describe the purpose of the focus group, selection criteria, and processes used.

Media options: During this step, the project team begins to look at learning styles and at matching media with learner requirements. Not everyone learns in the same way. People learn through visual, auditory, kinetic, or tactile means. The project manager may want to provide the project team with training in areas such as learner-centered instruction, distributed learning, learning styles, learning theory, instructional design, and accelerated learning. If so, the team should list these under the reference materials section of the form.

The project team may want to identify several training options, such as instructor-led, computer-based, linear video, and CD-ROM training. Table 6 describes media options, equipment and facilities needed for each, and interactivity. The more description the form provides into team members' thought processes and procedures, the more value the form provides as a model for later projects.

Key contacts: In this section, the team lists people whom they used as resources or could use as resources, whether inside the organization or external to it.

Recommendation: This is the only required section on this form. State the options and the result of analysis of research conducted here. The project team should make its recommendation either to purchase off-the-shelf courseware or develop an internal program.

Cost-center manager: The person with the purse signs off on this step. If that person is not the client, involve both.

Resources

The necessary resources for this step are as follows:

- **People:** The minimum roles for this step include a project manager; clerical, coordination, administrative support; client; subject matter expert; instructional designer; management; and course developer.

Table 6. Types of training available.

Type	Description	Inter-activity	Equipment	Facilities	Comments
Print based	Self-paced manuals. Students receive written learning package. May include audio and/or videocassettes.	Little	Duplication equipment, supplemental as needed	At-home workstation	Interactivity supplemental to media ie., e-mail, correspondence, or phone. Some institutes initiate study with on-site orientation; others allow open entry, open exit.
Audiotapes	Recording lessons on audiocassettes.	Little	Playback unit	At-home workstation	Interactivity supplemental to media
Audio	Linking one or more locations by telephone in live, interactive discussion	Moderate	Group conferencing equipment (speaker phone) Telephone transmission service Bridge	On-site conference room	Conference moderator with hard copy support materials
Audio plus graphics	Telephone-based system with visual enhancement	Moderate	Two systems, telephone and graphics at each location Tablets or writing boards, still video, fax	Separate telephone line for sending graphics, audio graphic equipment in each location	No compatibility among audio graphics systems conference moderator
Broadcast radio	Broadcasting pre-recorded lessons	Little	Broadcasting network Playback unit	At-home workstation	Interactivity through supplemental media

Continued on page 68

Table 6. Types of training available (continued).

Type	Description	Inter-activity	Equipment	Facilities	Comments
Videocassettes	Courses or supplemental course material put on videocassettes and distributed to students	Little	Playback	On-site room equipped with TV and VCR or at-home workstation comparably equipped	Interactivity through supplemental media
One-way video	Video program transmitted from one location to many receive sites	Little	Playback Downlink	On-site room equipped with TV and VCR or at-home workstation	Interactivity through supplemental media Conference moderator
Broadcast television	Video program broadcasted live	Little	Playback	Room equipped with TV and VCR	Interactivity through supplemental media
Two-way video	Distant sites equipped with ability to send and receive motion video as well as audio	High	Uplink, downlink	Room equipped with desks, camera and playback units	Conference moderator
Internet	Courseware delivery through World Wide Web.	High	Computer, modem, server	At-home workstation	Conference moderator with little control over organization or structure of interactions

Computer conferencing	Students receive instruction and interact with instructors and fellow students through computer	High	Computer at each site, software, modem and telephone line	At-home workstation	Conference moderator
Electronic mail	Personalized interactions between individuals and among groups who may be separated not only by distance but time	High	Computer, modem, software	At-home workstation	Little ability to structure or organize comments
Computer based	Use of computer in the instructional process in the form of drills and practice, tutorials, instructional games, modeling, simulation, and problem solving	Varies from low to moderate	Computer terminal connected to mainframe running presentation software; PC with software	On-site or at-home workstation	Up-front development time great Consultant used to develop or purchase courseware
CD ROM	Multimedia combination of CBT and interactive video	High	Computer equipped with CD drive	At-home workstation	Up-front development time great

- **Time:** The time required to complete this step depends on the learning curve of the team members, extent of review of off-the-shelf courses, number of people involved in review, and complexity of media.

- **Cost:** Costs may include people's time, registration fees for training, cost of reference material, charges for off-the-shelf courseware, hook-up fees for distributed learning, and travel.

- **Equipment:** Office automation software may include word processing, spreadsheet, and database as well as equipment and software for distributed courses.

Step 3 Case Study: Focus Group

During step 3 of TPPM, the Information Systems Department Training Unit of a large chemical manufacturer opted to involve customers in its training program research by including some of its internal customers, both champions and critics of its training program, in a focus group. Line managers nominated people, and the information system's management assisted in selecting group members.

The focus group consisted of customers from various departments, job positions, and skill levels. Because research and limited internal resources led toward outsourcing the delivery of the training, the focus group's charter was to select an external provider of training.

The project team defined contractual specifications, developed a Request for Proposal, and identified a number of local providers. The project team sent the Request for Proposal to those providers, and then compiled and analyzed their proposals. A short list of providers resulted.

The project team held an initial meeting of the focus group, explained the purpose, identified time frames, and answered questions. The project team used consensus building to identify criteria to evaluate the external providers. Criteria included elements related to learner-centered delivery, technology, instructional design, reliability of the provider, and ability to meet conditions identified on the Request for Proposal.

The focus group formed teams, targeted key courses for review, defined time frames, and selected providers. Ideally, teams took training together and someone who was knowledgeable about the subject matter was coupled with a novice. After attending the training, teams prepared a written review and distributed it to other members of the focus group. Once the focus group teams had completed their evaluation of the providers, the project team compiled the data and distributed them to the focus group. The project group held a meeting to discuss reactions and feedback. On the basis of the input from the focus group, the project team made its recommendation to outsource training.

6

Step 4:
Resource Allocation

During this step, the project team determines the costs of training and the benefits of training. Some organizations have standard formulas for determining training costs, but others do not, and their teams will face the dilemma of figuring out what to include. Costs may be direct (such as those for rooms or instructors), opportunity (such as those from missed sales or those gained in sales because of training), or productivity (such as costs of lost productivity during training or costs gained because of training).

Some items that companies typically consider when costing out training programs include the following:

- facility and room rent
- hardware and software
- equipment
- manuals
- development time
- salaries of instructor and learners
- food and other refreshments
- travel (instructor and learners)
- hours for training

- administrative and clerical support
- videos (purchased or made)
- duplication of videos
- printing of manuals
- licensing fees.

Project teams that choose off-the-shelf courseware may need to factor in these expenses:

- registration fees for the program
- registration fees for certification classes for trainers
- license fees for the program
- manuals, duplication, and copyright fees
- travel
- equipment
- access fees.

Benefits take the form of quantitative (that is, hard-dollar benefits) and qualitative (soft-dollar benefits). Examples of quantitative are the following:

- reduction in errors
- reduction in time
- increased productivity
- increased sales
- increased number of leads
- lower conversion rates
- increased number of customers
- increased "add on" sales
- fewer complaint calls
- increased number of people using system
- fewer calls to the help line
- increase in number of calls taken per hour.

This step is a critical point in the project—the go or no-go decision point for the project team and its client. In this step, the team analyzes the data that have been gathered and makes recommendations.

The form in figure 16 is a useful guide in working through this step. During step 4, the project team completes the project's budget. The projections and targets the team makes at this point determine the overall success of the project. These targets define whether or not the project will come in on time and within budget. The more accurately, reliably, and skillfully the project team predicts the final costs, the better the team can forecast the project results. This exercise develops skills and processes that members can transfer to other business activities.

Completing the Form

Project team: List the names of the people who participated on the project team. Remember, these people may vary from step to step.

Resource allocation: TPPM identifies this as a required section. The project team should provide estimates of the time, human resources, and materials needed to implement the training. The more educated the guesses are, the better. This exercise provides team members with an opportunity to develop skills in budgeting and in costing out projects, even if they are not training projects.

The table provides a means to summarize data. Project teams should feel free to tailor it to meet each project's individual needs. Table 7 shows an example of entries.

Time estimate: Under this required section, the project team establishes the time frame to complete the project. A Gantt chart or other similar tool can provide help in setting up the time frames.

Development costs: Project teams should always complete this section. In it, the project team itemizes the projected costs to develop the program. The team should take precautions to include all anticipated and hidden costs. The case study at the end of the chapter provides information on how a project team went about determining development costs for a project.

Figure 16. Training program resource allocation form.

Project Team: _____

_____

_____

Resource Allocation:
(Identify resources needed—materials, workers—to implement the training. Estimate the time needed for training program implementation.)

Resource	Time	Cost	Total ($)

Time-Frame Estimate:
(Estimate the amount of time for course development. Identify anticipated completion of the course.)

Development Costs:
(Estimate the costs to develop the training. Include human and equipment resources, audiovisual needs, publication of in-house training materials, external consultants, story-boarding, scriptwriting, video production, and so forth.)

Cost Justification:
(Estimate both the hard- and soft-dollar savings that the training will effect.)

Benefits:
(List benefits that company will derive from delivering the course. Identify costs of outside training, productivity gains, and the like.)

Cost-Center Manager: _____Date: _____

Cost justification: Under this section, the project team justifies the cost of the project. It identifies in quantifiable terms how the savings afforded by the training offset its cost.

To justify the costs of training, the team might consider such things as lost opportunity costs, costs of not training, increases in volume, and productivity gains. Cost justification can include both hard- and soft-dollar savings that the training brings about.

Table 7. Sample resource allocation entries.

Resource	Time	Cost	Total ($)
2 curriculum designers (outsource)	20 hours/week for 5 weeks	$85/hour@20 hours/week per person	17,000
1 administrative assistant	40 hours/week for 10 weeks	$20/hour	8,000
1 project leader	40 hours/week for 12 weeks	$60,000/year	14,400
software/hardware to access Internet for participants	1 hour/workstation to install	$200/package $50/installation 100 workstations	25,000

Benefits: In this section, the project team lists benefits derived by the organization through the training. Some of the items that fall into this section include decreases in costs compared with attending outside workshops, productivity gains, reduction in errors, and decreases in the number of complaints and turnaround time.

Cost-center manager: A cost-center manager must sign off on this step to legitimize the project and approve the expenditures.

Resources

The necessary resources for this step are as follows:

● **People:** The minimum roles for this step include a project manager, clerical support, client, and management.

● **Time:** The time to complete this step depends on the level of sophistication of analysis required for costs and benefits.

● **Cost:** The costs may include people's time to prepare the analysis and computer time.

- **Equipment:** Office automation software may include word processing, spreadsheet, statistical analysis packages, and database. Project management software provides assistance for planning to the project manager during this stage. This type of tool assists in the generation of Gantt charts, defining time frames, identifying critical path, and setting goals and outcomes for each phase.

Step 4 Case Study: Development Costs

The Information Systems Department formed a project team to develop a training program for a new word-processing software it planned to implement. In the program resource allocation step of TPPM, a project team determined that the organization had no standard formulas for determining training costs. Although the department traditionally offered computer software training, no one had attempted to identify the costs involved.

The team agreed that this information was critical for the project. The project leader conducted a brainstorming session to determine what might be related to program development costs. The team came up with this list of possible costs:

- computer time
- time for course developers
- time for participants in the pilot
- time for focus group meetings
- food
- time for instructor
- time for administrative support
- printing
- graphic design
- software
- facility costs
- presentation system
- transparencies
- reference materials
- training sessions for project team members.

The members determined that most of the items on the list related to time. In discussing the costs of their time as project team members, they determined that their time was billed out on a project basis to the rest of the company. Because this project was not their job, not for a specific department, and not billable, they needed to prioritize their tasks to make time for this added responsibility. The team agreed to use the allocation rate for assigning hourly costs. The analysts billed out at $40 per hour; the group assigned the rate of $20 per hour for administrative support.

After the brainstorming session, the group eliminated, consolidated, and grouped the items. They assigned costs to each item and came up with this list.

- administration
  —coordination (2 hours @ $20/hour)
  —scheduling (1 hour @ $20/hour)
  —enrollment (1 hour @ $20/hour)
  —ordering materials (2 hours @ $20/hour)
- materials
  —printing (transparencies $100)
  —graphic design (1 person, 5 hours @ $40/hour)
  —participant manuals (20 manuals at $3 per manual)
  —collateral materials (20 manuals at $5 per reference book)
- development
  —people (5 people, 30 hours per instructional hour @ $40/hour)
  —pilot (8 participants, 3 contact hours, 1 debrief hour @ $40/hour).

7

Step 5: Instructional Design

Step 5, instructional design, deals essentially with course design, pairing learners and instructional strategies that enable exit competencies. This step elaborates information identified in the form for step 2, program design. During the step, the project manager refines the parameters for the program and addresses the learning event, learner performance, and evaluation elements of the instructional model. The project team designs instructional strategies, develops learning materials, and specifies delivery medium. The training program instructional design form appears in figure 17.

During this critical step, the project team makes decisions about instructional strategy and instructional delivery. These decisions include the sequences and methods of instruction to achieve the program's learning objectives, and they guide course development. An effective instructional strategy prompts or motivates learners to actively associate what they already know with new information. It also helps learners to transfer new learning to their jobs and apply it in the workplace. Additionally, the instructional strategy helps to decrease the learning curve and aid in learners' retention.

The project team's decisions about instructional delivery describe the general learning environment. The learning environment can range from information centered to learner centered. In an information-centered environment, learners play a primarily passive role, whereas learners in a learner-

Figure 17. Training program instructional design form.

Project Team: _____
_____
_____

Course Code:
(Identify code or name assigned to the course.)

Learning Objectives:
(List learning objectives for the course.)

Modules:
(Identify the number of modules and their length.)

Class Size:
(State the minimum and maximum number of students recommended to participate in the class at one time.)

Organizational Range:
(Define whether participants should be intact departments, participants should come from horizontal or vertical slices, and whether supervisors should attend the same class that subordinates do.)

Frequency:
(Identify the number of times the class should be offered and how often.)

Cost:
(State the anticipated cost per participant.)

Length:
(Identify course length.)

Media:
(Identify media for the course delivery as well as audiovisual requirements.)

Hardware and Software Requirements:
(List special hardware and software requirements and setups needed to deliver the course.)

Course Outline:
(Identify topics included in the course. When doing this outline, keep in mind the number of modules and their length. Break the outline into appropriate sections to fit into session length.)

Project Leader: _____Date: _____

centered environment get actively involved in the learning, as table 8 shows. In a learner-centered environment, the facilitator applies many of the principles of adult learning.

During the instructional design step, the project team needs to consider how it will reach people because of their various learning styles. Some people learn visually; some auditorily; some tactilely; and some kinetically. In addition, learners bring other style preferences to the table. Instruments such as the Myers-Briggs Type Indicator, Kolb Inventory of Learning Styles, Gregoric Transaction Ability Inventory, and Grasha-Riechmann provide insight into learning styles. To reach learners and facilitate learning, course design should incorporate techniques that address different learning styles.

A further refinement made in this step classifies the level of individualization. Individualized instruction presents the content (or objective) to each learner at an appropriate rate for the individual. The typical lecture course provides an example of a nonindividualized approach.

If the project team sets as objectives to address learning styles, provide for a learner-centered environment, and provide for individualization, it is likely that learners will retain more, decrease their learning curve, and transfer skills to the job. The project team might involve focus groups again for their input and recommendations.

During this step, the project team defines and makes recommendations on such logistical considerations as the class sizes, audience, length, media requirements, classroom setup, and frequency for the classes.

Completing the Form

Project team: In this section, list all the members who participated as members of the team during this step. Again team members will vary from step to step.

Course code: Some organizations develop coding schema for their courses, others provide principles for course names, and still others give no guidance and thus have no consistency. During this stage of the project, the team should finalize the course title according to its organization's procedures and refer to the program by this title.

Table 8. Comparison of an information-centered environment with a learner-centered one.

	Information Centered	Learner Centered
Design	To cover all points; convey a lot of information; adhere to the lesson plan	To change behavior (improve the performance) of the learner
Underlying focus	Recognition of instructor's expertise	To meet learner's needs; improve performance
Role of instructor	To impart information; expert lecturer; "sage on the stage"	To arrange experiences and activities; moderate; "guide on the side"
Method	To talk; show and tell; instructor does 95 percent of the talking	Socratic—instructor asks questions and does no more than 50 percent of the talking
Typical questions	Do you have any questions? Do you understand?	Why do we do it this way? What would you do if...?
Learner's role	Passive—a sponge who absorbs information and periodically repeats it to give the instructor feedback	Active—learn by doing. Learners correct their own behavior because they are experiencing the results of their own actions
Purpose of feedback (or tests)	To see if learner understands the information; test the learner's retention; see if information should be repeated	To see if learner can apply what was just acquired; see if learner needs more practice; provide additional (remedial) instruction
How instructor gets feedback	By asking learners if they have any questions; by asking learners to repeat (often by rote) what instructor has just explained	By giving learners tasks or situations in which they must practice and apply their newly acquired skills, concepts, procedures, rules, and the like

Classroom management	Reward and punishment (sanctions and embarrassment)	Positive and negative reinforcement (praise and constructive criticism)
Instructor's expertise	The expert who knows more about the procedure, system, rules, and the like, than anyone else	The facilitator and guide; the moderator and coach who acts as catalyst
Instructor's basic philosophy	"There's so much our learners have to know before they'll ever be able to do the job correctly (that is, before they'll ever know what I know). Much repetition is necessary."	"We learn, not by being told, but by experiencing the consequences of our own actions. Learning is an experiential process; we learn by doing."

Learning objectives: During this step, the project team defines and specifies the learning objectives for the program. It states objectives for each module and verifies that the information chunking done earlier still makes sense. Following the instructional model described in chapter 4, the project team should define the learning objectives based on the established performance criteria determined during step 2. Again, the team needs to verify that the performance criteria still make sense.

The project team should write the learning objectives in behavioral terms. Teams that are not familiar with writing learning objectives can check numerous resources for guidance (see, for example, Gronlund, 1995; Mager, 1984).

General rules for generating the learning objectives include the following:

- Start with an action verb.

- Describe observable performances that learners will be able to achieve in relation to the outcomes of the program.

- State acceptable performance level.

- Include the conditions under which the action takes place.

The project team also needs to consider such things as learning domains and levels of learning, both of which figure in the development of learning events and in assessment of performance.

The project team should group learning objectives by a common thread or domain. Domains of learning include the cognitive, psychomotor, and affective. The cognitive domain deals with intellectual or knowledge outcomes. The affective domain addresses outcomes in the areas of interests, attitudes, and appreciation. The psychomotor domain applies to motor skills.

Objectives written for the cognitive and psychomotor domains reflect the structural side of Kotter and Hesket's (1992) model. These objectives refer to tasks accomplished. Objectives written for the affective domain reflect the cultural side and refer to behaviors. When the project team generates the learning objectives, they tie into the performance model at the point of tasks and behaviors. Tasks and behaviors have a direct impact on the organization's results.

Levels of learning relate to the performance criteria. Over the years, educators categorized the domains into taxonomies, or levels of learning. These taxonomies classify learning that takes place within the domains into a hierarchical order, from simple to complex. The project team correlates these taxonomies with the levels established in the performance criteria of the instructional model. For the training to be effective, the team needs to write the learning objectives to the same level as the performance criteria.

Because the learning objectives represent a critical success factor in program development, project teams need to complete this section for each project.

Modules: Use this section to describe the number and length of the modules. During curriculum design in step 2, the project team identified the number, content, and sequence of the modules. Now the project team defines the modules specifically. The team might also find it helpful to write a brief description of each of the modules and include them in this section.

Class size: In this section, the project team defines the minimum and maximum number of people in each class. Someone once said that the only thing worse than a class that is too big is one that is too small. When classes are too big, learner interaction decreases. When a class is too small, learner interactivity decreases.

Class size affects both the quality of instruction and the cost of delivery. Some organizations set standards for class size. These standards typically vary with delivery media, level of interactivity, and course content. For example, an organizational guideline might read: 20 people in an instructor-led class, 10 people in a hands-on class, 15 people in an online class.

In addition to the effectiveness of the instruction, the project team needs to consider such administrative aspects of the course as the following:

- What is a cost-effective ratio of facilitator to students?

- What does the course cost to run?

- Do we want to make money on the course or break even?

- How many people do we need to train to recover the development costs?

To assist in the administration of the program, the team might identify a minimum and maximum range of the class size for the course. The ranges, based on the cost effectiveness to deliver the course, would derive from the cost justification worked out in step 4.

Organizational range: In this section, the project team defines the ideal demographics of the class. Should teams attend as a work unit? Should the class composition consist of horizontal or vertical slices? Should supervisors attend with subordinates? Should we group all supervisors together? Should there be a mixture of departments and functional areas? Should the class be homogeneous?

These represent just a few of the questions the team should answer to define the organizational range for the program. The project team should base its recommendations on logistical constraints as well as value added and quality of instruction.

Frequency: The project team suggests how often to offer the class—for example, once a year, twice a year, monthly. Frequency needs to take into consideration the audience size, availability, shifts, and departmental coverage. In addition, the team needs to factor in make-up sessions.

Cost: In this section, the project team determines the cost per participant. Determining factors include frequency of delivery, audience size, and class size.

Length: The project team may have specified the length of the course under the module section. If not, that information goes here.

Media: This section is for information on both audiovisual requirements to deliver the course and the media used for the course. Audiovisual requirements might include such things as

- overhead
- TV/VCR
- CD player
- tape player/recorder
- flipchart
- camera
- screen
- whiteboard.

Media for the course might include

- diskettes for learners to store exercises temporarily

- diskettes that contain class exercises

- CDs that contain courseware

- videotapes for viewing vignettes

- videotapes for taping learner presentations.

Hardware and software requirements: The project team should use this section to specify hardware and software requirements to deliver the course. The descriptions should include networking capabilities and the connectivity the course requires. The team might choose to identify minimum requirements as well as the ideal.

Resources

The necessary resources for this step are as follows:

- **People:** The minimum roles for this step include a project manager; instructional designer; course developer; subject matter expert; clerical, administrative, and coordination support; client; and management.

- **Time:** Time depends greatly on the complexity and customization of the courseware being developed.

- **Cost:** Costs may include people's time, licensing fees, and registration fees.

- **Equipment:** Office automation software includes word processing, spreadsheets, and database. If the program uses multimedia courses, then authoring systems, online access, and video production will be necessary.

Step 5 Case Study: Instructional Design

Management in a midsized organization frequently used its supervisory personnel to deliver training programs to staff. The organization valued the use of its supervisors to deliver training programs, believing this practice offered a vehicle for development of the supervisors and improvement of communications and learning in the company.

These supervisors who served as facilitators had little if any background in either teaching or training. Often their classes turned out to be totally lecture based. Participants did not transfer skills to the workplace and often did not even show up for their sessions. When questioned, participants stated that the sessions were boring and that they didn't get anything out of attending.

Management realized that those supervisors needed training in training techniques. After doing a needs assessment, a project team identified these primary areas for training:

- adult learning
- learning styles
- training techniques.

Members of the project team agreed that they needed both to model a learner-centered approach when they delivered the training and to provide training in a learner-centered approach. In addition, the team wanted to individualize the delivery and address various learning styles. The team would learn about the topics, apply them in the design of the training course, and through the instructional strategies, transfer them to course participants.

To succeed in learning and modeling these approaches, the team agreed that it needed to allow time in the workshop design for activities and practice. In addition, the team agreed that consistency of delivery was one of its objectives. The members, therefore, chose to use a highly scripted approach to the leader's guide. The team agreed to put the workshop topics into a sequence in which each one built upon another. Participants would use skills gained in one module during the next.

8

Step 6: Training Program Instructional Development

Step 6 requires a lot of writing, attention to detail, and dedication. In this part of the process, the team develops the course or courses and the support materials, including the instructor's guide, administrator's manual, participant guide, and all collateral course material.

Before course development begins—in fact, before the project manager can begin using the training program instructional development form—he or she needs to reach consensus with the team on course development standards. These standards make up the guidelines the team agrees to follow to ensure consistency in the training courses, including all relevant print material. The guidelines may include such things as the following:

- margins
- capitalization
- spacing
- format
- level of interactivity
- approach, information versus learner centered
- visual aids
- degree of scripting

- checklists

- job aids

- paragraph levels

- writing style, such as active versus passive

- use of graphics

- type of numbering; such as roman numerals

- use of headers and footers

- software, version and level

- hardware

- lesson plan format

- centering

- frequency of learning activities

- frequency of breaks

- identification of when to use visual aids, do a learning activity, administer an assessment

- instruction on how to conduct learning activities.

Project teams that establish guidelines at the outset can increase their productivity and save time by reducing duplication of work and rework, eliminating questions, and producing consistent output. Figure 18 provides a sample set of course guidelines.

These guidelines establish the format for writing and production of the manuals and learner support materials developed in the training program instructional development step. By setting these guidelines early in the project, the project team is able to write manuals and generate support materials independently of one another and still have all the parts of the training program look and feel the same.

The agreement on guidelines thus provides a tool for team building for the project team. Although agreement on guidelines does not appear on the form, the project manager can use the activity to facilitate the processes of instructional development.

Figure 18. Sample set of guidelines.

MANUAL GUIDELINES

Headings	**VERY LARGE** **ALL CAPS** **BOLD** **CENTERED** **TRIPLE SPACE AFTER**
Side Headings	**LARGE** **ALL CAPS** **BOLD** **DOUBLE SPACE BEFORE** **SINGLE SPACE AFTER**
Paragraph Headings	**Bold** **Upper/lower case** **Double space before** **Single space after**
Titles	*Italic*
Optional Activities	OPTIONAL in caps and underlined Directions not underlined
Footer	File name, revision date, page number
Format	Cover sheet Objectives Materials Transparencies Power Point Presentation Handwritten Flipchart Titles Handouts Debrief Cards Visual Aids Supplies Step Page Instructor's Reference Activities Instructor Notes Transparencies Transition
Font	Times New Roman 12
ICONS	Large Gray Triple before and after
Action Steps	Numbers

Continued on page 94

Figure 18. Sample set of guidelines (continued).

Icons Used in the Instructor's Guide

These icons appear throughout the Leader's Guide to reference key support materials:

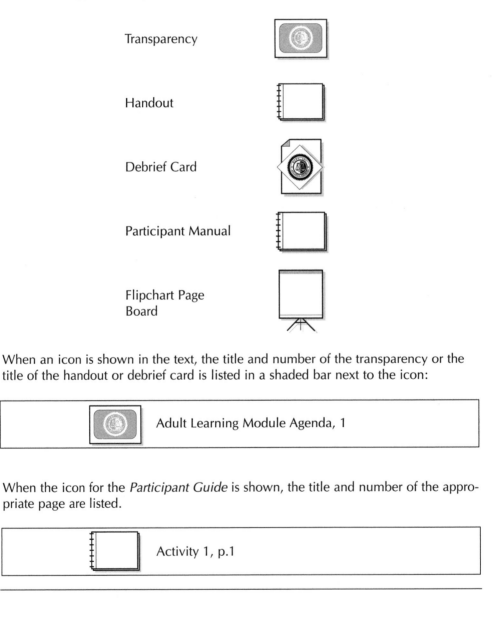

Transparency

Handout

Debrief Card

Participant Manual

Flipchart Page
Board

When an icon is shown in the text, the title and number of the transparency or the title of the handout or debrief card is listed in a shaded bar next to the icon:

Adult Learning Module Agenda, 1

When the icon for the *Participant Guide* is shown, the title and number of the appropriate page are listed.

Activity 1, p.1

As the project team develops courses and media during this step, it does a formative evaluation of them. To ensure quality before putting the entire course together, the team should test the modules as they're created. The team may choose to involve customers in the pilots at this point to gain their buy-in for the program and to avoid costly remakes of the course at a later time.

For courses that involve media, it will be necessary to create storyboards, write scripts, produce tapes, burn CDs, and develop a site-coordinator's manual as well as any other media and support materials. Generally speaking, the higher the level of technology involved, the longer the development time and the more expensive the program. After completing this step, the team has, in essence, completed the course.

The training program instructional development form appears in figure 19.

Project team: This section contains the names of the people who participated on the project team for this step. The names of the members of the project team may vary from step to step.

Instructor's manual: These guides become critical to the success of programs in which there are classes that are delivered several times, involve several different facilitators, or are held at several locations. For courses that might only be delivered once, instructor's guides and administrator's guides serve a lower priority.

If the project team elected to use off-the-shelf courseware, the team might write an explanation and attach samples of a purchased manual to the form for historical purposes. If the project team chose to outsource development, it should document discussions, agreements, and materials the consultant developed.

Before beginning to develop the courseware, the project team must reach consensus on philosophical intent, including the degree of freedom for the instructor, level of scripting in the manual, and level of learner interactivity. Some teams choose to provide detailed instructions to facilitators in the manuals, whereas others provide detailed outlines. Some teams strive for a high level of consistency in the delivery of the program, whereas others set as their goal the learner's attainment of exit competencies. Some teams include teaching strategies to promote a learner-centered approach to instruction, whereas others provide only course content in the manual.

Figure 19. Training program instructional development form.

Project Team: _____

_____

_____

Instructor's Manual:
(Attach hard copy or diskette originals for instructor's manual. Attach a list of the standards or guidelines used in development.)

Storyboard:
(Attach hard copy or diskette originals of storyboards.)

Script:
(Attach the scripts for videotapes or audiotapes.)

Media Development:
(Attach hard copy originals for development of media.)

Administrator's Manual:
(Attach hard copy or diskette originals for an administrator's manual. Attach checklists for implementing the course.)

Participant Manual:
(Attach hard copy or diskette originals for a learner's manual. Attach a list of the standards or guidelines used in development.)

Coordinator's Manual:
(Attach hard copy or diskette originals for a coordinator's manual. Attach technology requirements and specifications.)

Course Description:
(Describe the course. This information will go into a corporate training catalog to inform potential participants about the course. Include major topics covered as well as objectives if other than previously stated.)

Project Leader: _____Date: _____

Figure 20 shows excerpts from an instructor's manual for an organization that strives for high consistency in the delivery of its programs.

Storyboard: If the program uses media requiring the generation of storyboards, the project team should include a hard copy and perhaps diskette containing the storyboards. Documentation covering the reasons for, concepts covered, and discussions about the storyboard also prove helpful.

Figure 20: Excerpts from an instructor's manual.

TEAM (COMMITTEE) PROCESS

EXCERPT ONE: PRELIMINARY INFORMATION

OBJECTIVES:

At the conclusion of this module, participants will

- use brainstorming to generate ideas
- use consensus building to reach a group decision
- write a team agreement for their committee
- integrate charter and scope into committee process.

MATERIALS:

Transparencies
 "All for One & One for All"
 Workshop agenda
 Workshop objectives
 Brainstorming
 Consensus-building highlights
 Plus/Delta highlights

Handwritten Flipchart Titles
 Expectations
 Brainstorming
 Our team agreement
 Plus/Delta

Handbook
 Meeting Cookbook Handout

Debrief Card
 "All for One & One for All"
 Committee agreement

Supplies
 Mr. Sketch markers
 Tape
 Push pins
 Name tents
 Black markers
 Stopwatch
 Buzzer (optional)
 Candy (optional)

Continued on page 98

97

Figure 20: Excerpts from an instructor's manual (continued).

EXCERPT TWO: MEETING OUTLINE

STEP 1: Opening (15 minutes)

- Welcome faculty to the module
- Lead group through "All for One & One for All" ice-breaker
- Discuss workshop agenda
- Distribute faculty meeting handout

STEP 2: Overview (5 minutes)

- Discuss workshop objectives
- Discuss faculty expectations

STEP 3: Committee Process Utensils (45 minutes)

- Use brainstorming to generate group agreement for workshop
- Use consensus building to accept items on agreement
- Write a committee agreement
- Discuss a committee charter/charge

STEP 4: Wrap up (10 minutes)

- Summarize key points
- Identify module "take backs"
- Conduct a Plus/Delta
- Preview Meeting Module

EXCERPT THREE: DETAILED GUIDELINES FOR STEP 1

STEP 1: Opening (15 minutes)

Introduce yourself. Share information about your
    job function
    previous work experience
    time with organization
    involvement with committees, meetings.

Give administrative details; for example,
    workshop times
    numbers, times for breaks
    location of restrooms, fire exits, phones
    handling of messages

Distribute the *Meeting Cookbook* handout.
    Tell the participants that the handouts provide information and
      tools to help them run meetings more effectively.
    Walk participants through the sections of the handout

Continued on page 99

Figure 20: Excerpts from an instructor's manual (continued).

EXCERPT FOUR: EXERCISE DESCRIPTION

What is the "All for One & One for All" icebreaker?

This exercise helps to build a climate of friendliness and informality. It gives faculty members an opportunity to get to know one another, share information, and begin to work together. It serves as a foundation for team building and committee work.

Each person on a team has a distinct personality, qualities, and credos by which he or she lives. Each possesses both obvious and hidden strengths. In order to successfully work together, team (committee) members often need to know and call upon each other's special strengths and values. This exercise serves as a way for team members to get to know each other better as total personalities.

How do I conduct the exercise?

1. Create your personal coat of arms before the workshop to use as a sample.
2. Ask participants to turn to page 3 in the Team (Committee) Process section of their *Meeting Cookbook.*
3. Ask participants to design their own coat of arms according to this key:
    • Write something you excel at doing.
    • Draw a picture representing a one-time peak performance.
    • Write your credo or the key value by which you live.
    • Draw a symbol of your favorite leisure activity.
    • Describe in words one of your hidden qualities.
4. Display your premade Coat of Arms and discuss.
5. Give participants five minutes to design their Coat of Arms.
6. Break group into triads by counting off A, B, C.
7. Tell As to hold up their Coat of Arms. Bs and Cs comment on or ask questions about areas of the Coat of Arms. Give two minutes.
8. Rotate with Bs and Cs holding up their Coats of Arms and others commenting or questioning areas.

What are potential problems and limitations?

• Triads can get off track.
• Participants may be unwilling to share information.
• The exercise bogs down.
• Everyone knows one another.
• The exercise may be viewed as a time waster.

How Do I Debrief the Exercise?

Ask the participants these questions:
• What did you learn about members in your triads?
• What similarities or differences did you discover that you didn't know before?
• Why do this type of exercise?
• What areas had the greatest impact on you?
• How do you feel about your involvement in the group?

Script: If the program includes video- or audiotapes, the project team should attach a copy of the scripts in this section. Again, the project team might want to include brief summaries of the concepts covered, reasons for inclusion of specific material, and discussions about the material contained on the tapes.

Media development: If the program includes media, the project team should attach copies of the photos, transparencies of slides, and the like. This form serves as a good place to store originals for future use and reference.

Administrator's manual: This section provides information on the generation of a manual or checklists for the people to use who administer the course. Some items the team might choose to include in the manual are

- information on ordering materials
- names of internal and external contacts
- samples of confirmation letters
- samples of certificates of completion
- instructions on loading software
- room layouts
- audiovisual requirements
- room sizes
- class sizes
- special needs.

Participant manual: This is the only required section on the form. It contains samples of handouts, manuals, or support materials used in the delivery of the program. The team might want to attach a copy of the guidelines it created for the generation of the manual.

Coordinator's manual: Although similar to the administrator's manual, this manual is for site coordinators for programs delivered through distance learning. The coordinator's manual might include information on these topics:

- room size
- room setup
- hardware, software, and connectivity requirements

- support numbers
- information on ordering materials
- instructions on loading software
- instructions on operating equipment
- instructions on setting up user profiles
- instructions on responsibilities during workshop
- information on copyrights.

Course description: The project team can use this section to write a brief description of the course. This description can be used in promotional material about the course, course catalogs, and public relations. The manual might also include a listing of exit competencies, potential audience, and outcomes.

Resources

The necessary resources for this step are as follows:

- **People:** The minimum roles for this step include a project manager, course developer, subject matter expert, instructor and facilitator, clerical support, and client.

- **Time:** The time to complete the step depends on the complexity of the intervention under development. Traditional classroom sessions take less development time than multimedia ones.

- **Cost:** The costs may include people's time, access fees for conferencing, printing, graphics, rental of production facilities, production staffs, video or audio production, and fees for burning CDs.

- **Equipment:** Office automation software may include word processing, spreadsheets, graphics packages, and databases. If the program contains multimedia courses, the necessary equipment may include video production items, playback machine, and CD player.

9

Step 7: Training Program Implementation

In this step, the project team develops an action plan for implementing the training. This plan details how the project team will introduce, track, monitor, and evaluate the training intervention.

This step generally involves a pilot test of the course as well as a schedule for revisions that the project team identifies through a summative evaluation. Typically, the goal for summative evaluation of the pilot focuses on improvements, which the project team can make in the intervention before it finally releases the program. The evaluation usually consists of open-ended questions to solicit feedback from participants. Some project teams get the feedback from focus groups so they can piggyback responses with probing statements. The sample formative evaluation in figure 21 provides the type of questions project teams can use as conversation starters with a focus group.

In addition, the form should contain an evaluation plan for the program. The program evaluation in actuality consists of a plan within the plan.

Donald Kirkpatrick (1994) has identified the following four levels for training program evaluation:

- Level 1 is learner reaction.
- Level 2 is learning.

Figure 21. Sample formative evaluation form.

COURSE NAME _____   DATE _____

NAME (optional) _____

1. What are the strengths of the workshop?

2. What would you have liked to have been done differently in the course?

3. Name one thing you liked about the workshop.

4. What one thing would you change?

5. Comments

- • Level 3 is application.
- • Level 4 is results.

Over the years, these levels have become a standard in training and development for program evaluation. Learner reaction typically consists of smile sheets, which may be open- or close-ended questions, soliciting participants' perception of the training. Open-ended questions provide more qualitative comments; closed, more quantifiable.

Many organizations make use of a Likert scale in their evaluations. These organizations can tally the responses to get numerical information on the course.

Facilitators can assess learning in several different ways. A common way is through testing, such as pre- and posttesting, capstone application, or an exercise at the completion of the training.

Evaluation at the application level involves performance on the job, which organizations may measure through observation, follow-up questionnaires, or focus groups. As training and development move more toward performance improvement, evaluation at this level becomes more critical.

Evaluation at level 4 links the training to organizational results. What effect did the training have on the bottom line? Level 4 presents a challenge for most organizations. As project managers identify outcomes in step 2 of TPPM, evaluation at this level will become easier.

Many organizations evaluate at the level of learner reaction, some test, still fewer evaluate at the application level. Very few organizations reach the level 4 evaluation.

In addition to these levels, many organizations evaluate programs on an activity basis, identifying such things as the number of programs delivered, the costs, the number of participants, learner and instructor ratios, no-shows, and time in class. Together with Kirkpatrick's model, there are five levels for program evaluation. Table 9 summarizes these levels and the target audience for each type of evaluation.

Table 9. Five levels of program evaluation.

Level	Description	Assessments	Audience
1	Activity	Statistical Reports	Training Management
2	Learner Reaction	Course Evaluation Sheet	Training
3	Learning	Pre-Post Test	Participant
4	Application	Follow-up Questionnaire, Observation	Participant Supervisor
5	Business Results	Line Items Affecting Organization's Profit	Line Management

An example of one organization's program evaluation plan to reach level 5 appears in the case study at the end of this chapter.

The training program implementation plan form for this step appears in figure 22.

Completing the Form

Project team: A list of the members of the project team goes in this space. As members of the team change from step to step, make sure you give the names of all the people who participated as members of the team during the implementation plan.

Figure 22. Training program implementation plan form.

Project Team: _____

_____

_____

Implementation Schedule:
(Attach schedule and plan for implementation. Include location, trainer, target partici-pants, equipment needs, times, dates.)

Pilot Test:
Participants:
(List names and department of those people who participated in the pilot test for this course.)

Name   Department

Formative Evaluation:
(Attach evaluations from pilot test and notes. List any improvements to be made, how they will be done, and target date for completion.)

Improvements	Method	Responsible	Test Completion	Completion

Administrative Procedures:
(Identify procedures administrator follows for delivering program. State information, track-ing and reporting method administrator needs to follow.)

Measurements:
(Describe measurements)

Evaluation:
(State forms of summative evaluation.)

Project Leader: _____Date: _____

Implementation schedule: The project team identifies the plan for the program rollout in this section. The team should include in the plan informa-tion such as the following:

- locations
- facilitators

- target audience
- number of sessions
- equipment needed
- room requirements
- times and dates of sessions
- number of people to be trained
- make-up sessions planned
- contingency plans.

The project team is required to complete this section of the form.

Pilot test: A description of any pilot tests go in this section. The description should include information on participants, forms of analysis conducted, results of assessments, evaluation, revisions planned, and a schedule for revision.

Formative evaluation: If the team conducted a pilot, its action plan for revisions goes in this section. The columns in figure 23 are a sample of the information the team may wish to include. It includes space for members' suggestions of improvements to be made, how they will be made (for example, need more application rather than just description), the person or persons responsible for them, the date of a second pilot test, and the date of its completion. The project team should feel free to tailor the chart to fit its particular needs.

Administrative procedures: The project team may have covered this information in step 6 under the administrator's manual. If the team did not include information on that form or if the administration changes, the team should include the information in this section.

Measurements: The project team needs to define what measurements to use for the program. These definitions aid in the development of an evaluation plan, identify success, and bring closure to the project.

Evaluation: This section may involve a plan within a plan. The implementation form covers rollout of a program and may be all that is needed if the program is a one-time delivery. If the program is ongoing, the project team should probably develop a plan for continuous monitoring and evaluation. This plan defines summative evaluation for the project.

Resources

The necessary resources for this step are as follows:

- **People:** The minimum roles for this step include a project manager; course developer; instructor or facilitator; clerical, coordination, and administrative support; and the client.

- **Time:** The time involved depends on the length of the intervention and the revisions required.

- **Cost:** The costs may include people's time, access fees for conferencing, and travel.

- **Equipment:** The office automation software may include word processing, spreadsheets, and databases. If the course requires multimedia support, equipment might include such things as a CD player, PCs, terminals, video or audio playback units, overhead presentation units, overhead projectors, whiteboards, and electronic whiteboards.

Step 7 Case Study: Evaluation Plan for Legal Nurse Consultant Distance Education Project

During strategic planning sessions, an educational organization decided to convert one of its existing instructor-led programs to a distance learning format. The program offered students a certificate upon completion of approximately 24 courses over 18 months. The course delivered expected outcomes, but because it appealed primarily to working adults, some of whom were in far-off locations and many of whom worked during the day, the institute felt it could reach more people through a distance learning format. It identified a project team to convert the program.

Because of the size of the project and its complexity, the project team chose to outsource the actual course development to subject matter experts. The team also agreed to convert courses a quarter at a time, offer the courses to the public after successful completion of a pilot, and target a starting date in 24 months. The pilot would run concurrently with the instructor-led program.

Because of the nature of the project, the need to work backwards from a targeted start date, and desire to define return-on-investment, the project team began working on parts of step 7 early on. It identified opportunities for evaluation on several levels, including the following:

- **Project**

    —Did the project meet its goals?

    —What results did the project achieve?

    —How long was payback?

    —What shelf life does the program have?

- **Program: Activity.**

    —How many students enrolled? Completed? How long to complete?

    —How many and what kinds of people have program resources available?

    —What level of uptime did the technology achieve?

    —Did the Internet access provider achieve the expected level of satisfaction?

—What training did the staff receive on technology?

—What training did the faculty receive on technology?

—What training did the students receive on technology?

—Did the program meet the needs and expectations of the target groups?

—What are the student demographics?

—What is the appropriate student-faculty ratio? What is the appropriate faculty workload?

- **Program: Reaction.**

—What level of customer satisfaction did the program achieve?

—What level of instructor satisfaction did the program achieve?

- **Program: Learning.**

—Do differences exist in student knowledge, skills, and attributes (KSAs) between traditional classroom and distance education delivery?

—Did students achieve exit competencies?

- **Program: Application.**

—Do curriculum exit competencies match job requirements?

—Can the students perform on the job?

—Did staff and faculty perform at the desired level of competency?

- **Program: Results.**

—What return-on-investment did the program produce?

—What kind of impact did the program have on the mission, goals, and practices of the organization?

—How cost-effective was the program?

—Did the program achieve acceptable level of profitability?

As part of its evaluation plan, the project team developed a chart (see case table 1) as a job aid to ensure evaluation of all aspects of the project development. The chart tracks for each of the project team member's roles the different aspects of the project that require evaluation.

Case table 1. Summary of types of evaluations, their audiences, and priority.

Audience	Description	Reasons for Evaluation	General Purpose	Priority
Instructional designer	Subject matter experts courseware review	Obtain feedback on content, scope, strengths, and weaknesses	Make improvements in quality and content; formative	1
Instructional designer	Focus group courseware review	Assess course quality and appropriateness	Make improvements in quality and content; formative	1
Sponsors	Pilot course	Determine if project on target and if funding should continue	Assess progress toward goals; formative	1
Faculty	Course by course	Obtain feedback on strengths, weaknesses, content, and delivery	Make improvements in quality and content; formative	2
Project team	Small group instructional diagnosis	Obtain feedback on strengths, weaknesses, content, and delivery	Make improvements in quality and content; formative	2
Faculty	Learner reaction	Assess customer satisfaction	Make improvements in program design, resource accessibility; formative for program, summative for course delivery	1
Project team	Faculty focus group	Assess faculty satisfaction	Make improvements in program design, resource accessibility; formative	1

Continued on page 112

Case table 1. Summary of types of evaluations, their audiences, and priority (continued).

Audience	Description	Reasons for Evaluation	General Purpose	Priority
Project team	Checklists, forms, logs, questionnaire	Obtain student support services information (that is, accessibility, communications, feedback, enrollment, grade reporting, time per student, number of student inquiries, number of faculty responses, course completion time)	Make improvements in work flow, work design, quality of program; formative	1
Faculty	Learner assessments	Evaluate student attainment of exit competencies and progress	Remediation Make improvement in program design, resource accessibility Formative, summative	1
Management	Reports	Report statistics related to program (that is, student enrollments, completion rate, placement); compare traditional to distance delivery	Track data; summative	2
Project team	Questionnaire focus group	Assess if program meets job requirements and students demonstrate KSAs	Make improvements in content; formative	1
Course developer	Course review	Obtain feedback on readability	Make improvements in readability; formative	2
Graphics designer	Course review	Obtain feedback on typographic style	Make improvements in page style; formative	3
Advertising	Market review	Obtain feedback on leads, conversions, cost per lead	Make improvements in advertising; target markets; formative	1

The *audience* column lists each role of one or more members of the project team, including the role of the entire team. *Description* lists the assessment tool, and reasons for the evaluation tell what is expected from it. The general purpose column identifies actions to take resulting from evaluation, and priority categorizes the value for the evaluation. The project team used this form for guidance through implementation of the project.

Instruments

The numerous evaluations during conversion of the program necessitated use of several data-gathering instruments. Because the pilot involved students, faculty, and course developers, the project team decided to administer the instruments to each group at the end of each quarter throughout the pilot. In this way, the project team could lead the revision of the previous quarter's courses, deliver finished courses to students, and oversee the writing of the next quarter's courses. Following are some of the instruments:

- **Checklists for courseware review by internal subject matter experts (SMEs).** These checklists (see case figure 1) helped to simplify and objectively represent feedback from SME when they completed their course review. The form provides for both quantitative and qualitative data. Questions 1 to 15 of the checklist use a Likert scale. The last question asks for a free-form, open-ended, section-by-section review of the courseware. After data compilation and reduction, the project leader reviewed the information with the consultant. The consultant then made the necessary revisions in the courseware.

- **Questionnaire for focus group courseware review.** The questionnaire (see case figure 2) helped guide courseware reviewers as they read print material. The focus group was made up of members of the project team and staff. The form provides for both quantitative and qualitative data, much the same as the checklist for SMEs. Questions 1 to 13 use a Likert scale, and the last question asks for a free-form, open-ended, section-by-section review of the courseware. The information was useful in revising course content, readability, and appearance. After data compilation and reduction, the project leader reviewed the information with the

Case figure 1. Course review checklist for subject matter experts.

	Excellent	Good	Average	Fair	Poor
1. Exit competencies relate to KSAs students will need on the job.	5	4	3	2	1
2. Learning objectives support the exit competencies.	5	4	3	2	1
3. Exit competencies are comprehensive.	5	4	3	2	1
4. Course material supports the objectives.	5	4	3	2	1
5. Courseware is correct.	5	4	3	2	1
6. Material is up-to-date.	5	4	3	2	1
7. All important topics are covered in the courseware.	5	4	3	2	1
8. Material avoids redundancy.	5	4	3	2	1
9. Course flows logically.	5	4	3	2	1
10. Course avoids oversimplification	5	4	3	2	1
11. Course avoids overgeneralization.	5	4	3	2	1
12. Course is balanced and recognizes opposing viewpoints, where appropriate.	5	4	3	2	1
13. Course presents concepts clearly.	5	4	3	2	1
14. Course contains satisfactory examples, analogies, and case studies.	5	4	3	2	1
15. Please do a section-by-section review, noting where material is weak, incomplete, or hard to follow. What further work is needed? Note any sections that are too long (possibly unfocused or repetitious) or too short (possibly underdeveloped).					

Case figure 2. Course review questions for the focus group.

	Excellent	Good	Average	Fair	Poor
1. Learners will understand what is expected of them.	5	4	3	2	1
2. Learners can achieve objectives.	5	4	3	2	1
3. Learner should be able to complete section within estimated time frame.	5	4	3	2	1
4. The material is at the appropriate level of difficulty.	5	4	3	2	1
5. The material is interesting.	5	4	3	2	1
6. Examples, analogies, and case studies seem relevant to learners' interests.	5	4	3	2	1
7. The course uses a variety of teaching techniques.	5	4	3	2	1
8. The course addresses a variety of learning styles.	5	4	3	2	1
9. All new terms are adequately explained.	5	4	3	2	1
10. The number and distribution of activities and self-assessments are appropriate.	5	4	3	2	1
11. The course maintains a consistent focus.	5	4	3	2	1
12. Clear transitions exist between sections.	5	4	3	2	1
13. The illustrations are interesting.	5	4	3	2	1

14. Please do a chapter-by-chapter review, noting where material is weak, incomplete, or hard to follow. What further work is needed? Note any chapters that are too long (possibly unfocused or repetitious) or too short (possibly underdeveloped).

consultant. The consultant then made the necessary revisions in the courseware.

● **Course-by-course questionnaire for student assessments of a pilot course.** These questions (see case figure 3) helped focus students' comments as they took each course in the pilot program. Upon finishing a course, students completed the questions and returned them anonymously to the faculty member. Faculty used the feedback as input for revisions in the course and discussed changes with the project leader. The project leader then discussed relevant content information with the consultant. The consultant made changes in later versions of the courseware. The project leader provided administrative staff with feedback related to student support services. Decisions centered around appropriate work process modifications.

● **Small group instructional diagnosis.** Case figure 4 offers a more formalized, interactive vehicle for feedback from students in the pilot course. Its responses were critical to the project team's decisions about beginning the training project.

The pilot design involved a control and an experimental group. The experimental group consisted of volunteers from the winter class. The

Case figure 3. Course-by-course questionnaire for students.

1. I feel the strengths of this course are

2. I suggest these changes for the next time the course is offered:

3. I received (did not receive) adequate support while completing the course. Here are some specific examples:

4. This course made me think about the following ideas:

5. The technology does (does not) work for me. Here are some specific examples:

Case figure 4. Small group instructional diagnosis.

1. What did you like about this course?

2. What do you think needs improvement?

3. How would you go about making these improvements?

4. Technology enhanced (detracted) from the course in these ways.

5. Training (support) in these areas helped (would have helped) me learn the course material.

---

control group consisted of the other students enrolled in the program. Which students were in the pilot course, therefore, hinged on the natural sequence of courses in the program. After completion of the pilot course, students from the experimental group rejoined students in the natural sequence of courses.

Students completed the small group instructional diagnosis (case figure 4) around the middle of the pilot course. All program participants in the pilot were invited to a one-hour meeting at the school. Because students would normally take classes on this campus, logistical difficulties of assembling the class and conducting the activity were minimized. To ensure anonymity, the project leader served as facilitator. During the meeting, the facilitator divided the group into smaller groups and asked them to discuss and then report to the large group on three questions. Students were given 20 minutes to discuss all the questions. At the end of the time, each group reported to the whole group. Time was available for large group discussion. Responses were typed, and the project leader discussed them with the instructor and consultant.

● **Student course evaluations.** At the completion of each course, students filled out and turned in a standard school student course evaluation. The project leader compiled and summarized responses from these forms.

- **Interview questions for faculty focus groups.** At the completion of the initial pilot course as well as each course in the pilot program, faculty participated in a focus group to provide input on their level of satisfaction with the delivery method. The process for conducting the focus groups was similar to that for the small group instructional diagnosis. Interview questions for these groups appear in case figure 5.

- **Student learning assessments.** Student learning assessments and evaluations vary with each course. The assessments parallel current assessments and evaluations used in the traditional delivery of the program.

Case figure 5. Interview questions for the faculty focus group.

1. What did you like about this course?

2. What do you think needs improvement?

3. How would you go about making these improvements?

4. Technology enhanced (detracted) from the course in these ways.

5. Training in these areas helped (would have helped) me function effectively.

- **Employer questionnaire, interview questions focus group.** We used two techniques to assess application of skills by students on the job. One addressed customer (employer) satisfaction with our students, and the other followed up on students to see if they were applying the new skills on the job. The customer satisfaction survey was an ongoing assessment. The follow-up survey of application of the skill on the job was a summative evaluation of the pilot program.

The ongoing technique consisted of the school's employer satisfaction form. It was for comparison with the benchmark achieved by the current class.

The second technique to assess the achievement of exit competencies by students in the pilot consisted of two components. One was a questionnaire that the employer completed on the skill application on the job (see case table 2), and the other was a series of interviews at a focus group meeting (see case figure 6).

- Reporting mechanisms for management. Management obtained the following information from appropriate mechanisms:

    —enrollment

    —retention

    —completion rates

    —placement

    —starting salary

    —student-teacher ratio

    —leads

    —conversion rate.

Case figure 6. Interview questions employer focus group.

1. What strengths do the graduates of the program demonstrate?

2. What areas of weaknesses do you think the graduates of the program have?

3. How do graduates of the Legal Nurse Consultant program compare with those of other distance education programs? _____
    those trained in the field? _____
    those of traditional programs? _____

4. Where do most beginning nurse consultants "fail" on the job?

5. Describe the characteristics, skills, competency level of the "ideal" legal nurse consultant.

6. What suggestions do you have for improving the quality of the graduates from the Legal Nurse Consultant program?

Case table 2. Skill application on the job.

Initials	Demonstrated on the Job	Not demonstrated on the job	N/A	Knowledge, Skills, Abilities
				Research legal and medical topics using text.
				Research legal and medical topics using on-line references.
				Review medical records.
				Recognize legal issues in medical records.
				Draft a report summarizing legal issues contained in medical records.
				Utilize computers to assist in job functions.

Analysis of Evaluation Data

Data analysis and reporting mechanisms varied with the instruments. Case table 3 summarizes the rationale, resources, and report form for each evaluation instrument.

Management and Reporting Plan

Evaluation occurred throughout the life of the project. We associated the evaluation instruments with the appropriate phase of the project as follows:

Phase	Evaluation Instrument
Development phase	SME courseware review Focus group courseware review
(Pilot course)	Small group instructional diagnosis Course by course Learner assessments/evaluation Learner reaction Faculty reaction
Implementation (pilot program)	Course by course Learner assessments/evaluation Learner reaction Faculty reaction
Evaluation	Management reports Customer satisfaction Employer questionnaire Employer focus group

After the completion of the pilot program, the project manager submitted a final report to project sponsors that summarized the information derived from the evaluations as well as project accomplishments.

Case table 3. Rationale, resources, and report form for each evaluation instrument.

Instrument	Analysis Technique	Rationale	Resources	Report Form
SME checklist	Averages—questions with Likert scale; data reduction—open-ended comments	Provides general indication of SME's responses; identifies broad areas for improvement; gives feedback on SME's comments section by section; provides insight into SME's perspective	SME, project leader, consultant, support staff, time, duplicating, phone calls	Written report, phone conversation
Focus group questionnaire	Averages—questions with Likert scale; data reduction—open-ended comments	Provides general indication of focus groups' responses; identifies broad areas for improvement; gives feedback on focus group's comments section by section; provides insight into focus group's perspective	Focus group, project leader, consultant, support staff, time, duplicating, phone calls	Written report, phone conversation
Student course-by-course questionnaire	Data reduction	Provides general comments from student's perspective	Students, faculty, project leader, consultant, support staff, time, duplicating, phone calls	Written report, discussion between faculty and project leader; phone conversation, project leader and consultant
Small group instructional diagnosis	Data reduction	Provides general comments from student's perspective	Students, project leader, consultant, support staff, time, duplicating, phone calls	Written report, phone conversation

Student course evaluations	Question-by-question averages	Provides general indication of learner reactions	Students, project leader, faculty, support staff, time, duplicating, phone calls	Written report, discussion with faculty, phone conversation with consultant
Student learning assessments	Examinations, class assignments, activities, projects	Grades	Students, faculty, project leader, time, processing	Grade reports
Employer questionnaire	Question-by-question averages	Provides general indication of application on the job	Graduates, employers, project leader	Written report
Employer focus group	Data reduction	Provides general comments from employer's perspective	Graduates, employers, project leader	Written report
Management reports	Percentage, averages, costs	Provides statistical data related to measurement	Project leader, dean of education, support staff, management, computer	Computer-generated reports
Gallup customer satisfaction survey	Standard deviation	Provides statistical analysis of customer satisfaction survey	Employers, Gallup, support staff, computer	Computer-generated reports

123

10

Step 8: Training Program Evaluation

When the team has completed this step, the course is completed and implemented. The project reached its end. In this step, the project team documents the project's success and attainment of the measurements identified in step 2. The training program evaluation step serves to focus the training on the business. Through this evaluation step, the team aligns its product with the product of the business. This activity helps bring line and training functions closer together. Watson (1998) states: "In practice, most failed measurement efforts lack a clear connection to the desired business outcomes." This step serves to provide that linkage.

During this step, the project manager evaluates the outcomes of the program implementation and reports on the results of the evaluation plan defined in step 7. The project team needs to summarize program costs, benefits, and conclusion, which it does through a summative evaluation. This evaluation brings the project to closure by tying together the earlier steps in which the project team identified training requirements and program goals. For all practical purposes, at the completion of this step, the project team disbands.

In general, training programs either provide solutions to immediate or one-time organizational needs, or they become part of an ongoing curriculum. If the course was developed to meet a one-time training need, the project and course terminate. If the training program becomes part of an ongoing schedule of offerings, however, the person responsible for managing, monitoring, and delivering the program gets identified.

When the project concludes, a key activity, often forgotten or omitted, is the celebration of the project. For the most part, when the team disbands, members do not celebrate the project's success; typically, members of the project team just go back to their "normal" jobs. This celebration, however, provides a critical step in the project. It brings closure to the project and a sense of accomplishment to the team. The form of celebration depends on the culture within the organization. Celebrations may take the form of a cake, T-shirts, party, lunch, dinner, or simply an e-mail from the project manager or sponsor thanking the members and congratulating them.

The entire team should also meet for a debriefing of the project. At this debriefing meeting, the team and stakeholders should review the project's successes, shortcomings, and learnings. These learnings include what the team, organization, and participants learned. The team should identify activities that went particularly well, things that did not go as planned but are worth trying again, and mistakes never to be repeated. The debriefing session helps imprint the team's learnings into the organization's history.

Organizations can, thus, use this project methodology to help move closer to becoming a learning organization. The project methodology incorporates learning at the individual, team, and organizational levels by providing a developmental opportunity to three audiences: participants in the program, participants on the project team, and the organization.

This last step, the training program evaluation, serves not only to bring closure to the project but also to link the training with the business. The training program evaluation form is in figure 23.

Completing the Form

Project team: A list of the members of the project team goes in this space. As members of the team change from step to step, make sure you include the names of all the people who were team members during the evaluation. Teams may wish to list everyone who participated on the project team

Figure 23. Training program evaluation form.

Project Team: _____

_____

_____

Summary of Program Costs:
(List actual versus budget expenses.)

Learners' Reactions:
(Attach copies of learner reaction sheets.)

Summary of Learning:
(Analysis of results of pre- and posttests, observation, and evidence of learning.)

Summary of Follow-up:
(Describe methods and results of follow-up.)

Summary of Implementation:
(Describe measure, for example, number of people trained and number of programs run.)

Summary of Benefits:
(Describe hard and soft benefits.)

Return-on-Investment:
(Describe quantitative methods used to analyze the return-on-investment.)

Cost-Center Manager: _____Date:_____

on this form throughout the project to serve as reference, documentation, or identification of people who participated in the debriefing session.

Summary of program costs: In this required section, the project team should itemize all the costs of the program. As a critical activity in this section, the team should compare the actual costs with the ones anticipated in step 4. This task serves to validate the project, measure success, and guide estimates in later projects. If the original estimates were out of line, the team should explain the differences and state recommendations, processes, or formulas to help future teams estimate program costs early in their projects.

Throughout the project, the project manager should track, monitor, approve, and audit expenditures. Project managers that do so will find this section much easier to complete. This section loses its value as a tool if project managers rely on their memory to complete it. Instead, they should track costs by setting up a simple spreadsheet or database, or by using software like Quicken or Quick Books. By recording, identifying, and tracking expenditures along the way, project managers can avoid getting blindsided, and they can answer questions posed by management related to budget. The project manager, furthermore, can identify whether or not the project came in within budget.

This step provides critical learning for the team and gives important training for the team on budgeting. The team members can transfer these skills not only to other training projects but also to other types of projects to which their organization may assign them.

Learner reaction: Learner reaction sheets represent a common form of summative evaluation for training programs. In these course evaluations, learners give their perception of what happened in the course and the value it added. The learners constitute the customer base; they do not necessarily possess knowledge of training principles, concepts, or theory. The project team, therefore, needs to put information gleaned from the learner reaction sheets into context.

Value from the learner reaction sheets also depends on the effectiveness of the design of the course evaluation form. The more effective the design, the more useful is the information it provides to the team. The course evaluation, therefore, should have specific objectives and gather information related to them. Unfortunately many trainers use questions from other course evaluations and pay little attention to the purpose of the question or of the evaluation in general. Thus, the data received do not provide meaningful information.

Several examples of objectives for the learner reaction sheet include the following:

- provide a diagnostic instrument
- identify blatant overall course deficiencies
- target areas for improvement
- assess aspects of training effectiveness, such as
  —instruction
  —content

—applicability

—involvement

—facilities

—delivery media.

Figure 24 shows a sample learner reaction sheet from a train-the-trainer program. The first group of questions ask learners their perception of how well the course objectives were met. The second section seeks information from the learner on the effectiveness of the course segments. The third section addresses the course delivery and lists questions relating to four aspects of training effectiveness: instruction, content, applicability, and involvement.

One of the challenges in designing a form is to make it both open enough that respondents will have an opportunity to comment and easy enough that project teams can compile and analyze data easily. This form provides for ease of compilation and both closed and open-ended questions.

Summary of learning: This section is optional. If completed, it should include a description of the learning that took place as a result of participants' attendance at the training program. The project team can give evidence of learning in several ways and at several levels. For example, the team can analyze the scores that participants made on pre- and posttests. This measurement addresses Kirkpatrick's level 2 learning. Another example of a measurement for level 2 learning might consist of an assessment of participant performance through in-class observation. Another example of level 2 learning would be a summary of participants' scores on mastery tests or a demonstration of the acquired skills through an in-class assessment or a videotape for later review and reference.

The team might also strive to measure learning at level 3, application. Examples of this level are an observation of participants on the job, statements of performance improvements on the job, or an identification of reduction in errors directly related to the training.

Summary of Follow-up: In this optional section, the project team describes methods used as follow-up to the training. Follow-up options available to the team include

- observations of participants once they return to their jobs

Figure 24. Sample learner reaction sheet.

Train-the-trainer workshop evaluation

We are interested in your assessment of this workshop. Please help us provide you with high-quality programs by responding to these items. Indicate your response to each item by circling the appropriate number.

COURSE OBJECTIVES: Indicate how well you believe each of the workshop learning objectives was achieved.

		Poor	Fair	Good	Very good	Excellent
1.	Define and explain concepts of adult learning.	1	2	3	4	5
2.	Compare and contrast principles of an information-centered approach with those of a learner-centered approach.	1	2	3	4	5
3.	Identify practices to apply in a workshop to support a learner-centered approach.	1	2	3	4	5
4.	Use Personality Type Inventory to assess individual personality type.	1	2	3	4	5
5.	Compare and contrast learning style differences in a workshop environment.	1	2	3	4	5
6.	Associate training styles to learning styles.	1	2	3	4	5
7.	Identify training techniques that support personality type preferences.	1	2	3	4	5
8.	Prepare an action plan to address learning style differences in a workshop environment.	1	2	3	4	5
9.	Describe critical elements of training techniques presented in the workshop.	1	2	3	4	5
10.	Select a training technique from those presented, design a 10-minute exercise based on individual course material, and deliver the exercise to participants in the workshop.	1	2	3	4	5
11.	Provide feedback to other participants on 10-minute training technique exercise delivery, effectiveness, and appropriateness.	1	2	3	4	5

COURSE SEGMENTS: Indicate how effective the information presented in each segment was for you.

		Very Ineffective	Somewhat Ineffective	Adequately Effective	Very Effective	Extremely Effective
1.	Learner-centered instruction	1	2	3	4	5
2.	Learning styles	1	2	3	4	5
3.	Training techniques	1	2	3	4	5
4.	Skill building	1	2	3	4	5

Continued on page 131

Figure 24. Sample learner reaction sheet (continued).

COURSE DELIVERY: Indicate the extent to which you agree or disagree with each of these statements.

	Strongly Disagree	Disagree	Neither Agree nor Disagree	Agree	Strongly Agree
1. I will be able to apply the information or skills provided in the workshop.	1	2	3	4	5
2. This workshop lived up to my expectations.	1	2	3	4	5
If not, what expectations were not met? _____					
3. Training materials and audiovisuals helped reinforce the key learning points.	1	2	3	4	5
4. The facilitator: a. explained the purpose of each activity and provided clear direction.	1	2	3	4	5
b. led productive and meaningful discussions	1	2	3	4	5
c. created a comfortable and open learning environment.	1	2	3	4	5
d. presented material at the right pace.	1	2	3	4	5

5. Please give examples of techniques facilitators used that you found helpful; or those that you did not find beneficial.

6. Please give suggestions of ways we can improve the workshop.

7. Please suggest future workshops you would like.

Additional comments.

- surveys distributed to participants several months after training to see how they are applying skills learned

- questionnaires sent to supervisors after participants have had time back on the job

- phone interviews with supervisors

- discussions with customers

- focus group meetings

- customer transaction records.

In this section, the team should include not only the method but also an analysis of the information derived from the follow-up. The team might want to summarize the data in the form of a chart for easy future reference.

Summary of implementation: In this optional section, the project team should describe the process used to analyze the program's implementation. The team should include the form of measurement of program success and the level the program attained. Items the team can list in this section include the number of people trained, the number of hours trained, the number of courses delivered, and the location of the sessions.

Summary of benefits: In this required section the team lists both quantitative and qualitative benefits derived from the program. The team should cost justify the training effort.

Return-on-investment: In this section, the team answers the question, "What did it cost to gain these benefits?" Although the section is optional, it provides critical information and aids in future training decisions. It is in this section that the team can reach level 4, evaluation. According to Watson (1998), "Together, line and training functions must dig deeply into the underlying forces that affect revenue, customer or client relationships, and business results. There are no shortcuts."

Watson (1998) further states, "Meaningful measurement requires collaboration. A strong focus on your organization's business issues provides a shared purpose and a sense of mission. It is the most fundamental reason for building a relationship between line and training functions."

Some examples of measurements include

- increase in revenue
- increase in new customer contacts
- presenting solutions
- increase number of sales closed
- decrease in downtime
- decrease in customer complaints
- increase in productivity
- reduction in errors
- fewer lost-time accidents.

Cost-center manager: The client should sign this form to add closure to the project.

Resources

The necessary resources for this step are as follows:

- **People:** The minimum roles for this step include a project manager; course developer; instructor or facilitator; clerical, coordination, and administrative support; client and management.

- **Time:** The time involved varies with project implementation. In this case, the team can specify time used for the initial implementation; or if the program is ongoing, the team might want to identify the time needed for coordination, administration, and delivery of the training course once implemented.

- **Cost:** The costs may include people's time.

- **Equipment:** The office automation software may include word processing, spreadsheets, and databases. Project management software provides assistance for analysis.

11

Summary

During the past few years, organizations have begun to realize that in order to succeed in today's market environment, they need to operate differently from the way they operated in the past. This holds true for individuals as well. Traditional ways of doing business are giving way to telecommunications, collaboration, partnerships, global markets, and other forms of out-of-the-box thinking. Organizations see teams as a way to gain the competitive advantage and team skills as critical for their employees. More and more, organizations are striving to become learning organizations to keep competitive. In this environment, the organization, teams, and individuals learn and grow.

Although people may tire of hearing about downsizing, right sizing, mergers, acquisitions, buyouts, consolidations, and takeovers, these have become a fact of life for U.S. organizations. To remain ahead of the curve, both organizations and individuals need to close the gap between current competencies and those required in the high-performance organizations of the future. Closing the gap requires willingness to upgrade skills, gain experience in new areas, and pursue lifelong learning.

Successful organizations of the future will provide opportunities for employees to gain marketable skills, and successful employees will remain marketable.

Training and development will, therefore, play a key role in the organizations, but it will need to work differently. Training and development (T&D) will, for example

- work in tandem with line managers. T&D functions will not be seen as a separate entity staffed with training professionals. Training will become part of the day-to-day operations and skill sets of the team leader.

- become transparent to the job. Employees will learn while they perform job functions. Team members will cross-train to pick up the ball for other team members.

- extend temporary assignments as individual developmental experiences. Employees will take on new responsibilities and transform as they learn. Team members will assume the role of project manager and guide projects as self-directed teams become commonplace.

- deliver learning "anytime, anywhere." To meet participants' needs, scheduling restrictions, and location requirements, training will turn increasingly to technology to deliver training.

- link evaluation to organizational results. Training will need to assess the value it provides using quantifiable measurements.

As organizations evolve into high-performance organizations and teams become prevalent, titles, positions, and responsibilities will change. Middle managers will take on more technical responsibilities. To remain marketable, middle managers will become more involved in operations and day-to-day work. They will need hands-on, technical training. Specialists will assume more management duties. These people need training on supervision and project management.

The role of the project manager will take on greater significance as middle management positions erode and teams become commonplace. As organizations do away with levels of middle management, team members gain opportunities to learn, assume more responsibility, and develop professionally.

As these "instant" managers emerge, they need support. What do they need? When asked, they said:

...they needed to acquire the "big picture" regarding the project management process, a framework for organizing the projects and guiding their activities. They also told us that these new project managers need simple, step-by-step guidance. They need to know what specific project management actions to take, when to take them, and how to know when they have achieved the appropriate results. (Greer, 1998)

How do they want support? Some examples of tools that training and development can provide include the following:

- checklists
- worksheets
- guidelines
- models
- manuals
- help sessions
- community of practice
- job aids.

TPPM was designed to serve as this guide to help training and development professionals bridge the gap to project manager. It is not a silver bullet for those responsible for managing training projects. Rather, its purpose is to provide guidelines, checklists, models, and worksheets that training project managers can use as aids in managing their projects.

Training project managers tailor these aids to the needs of their unique projects. Figure 25 provides a job aid to help the training project manager track and monitor the action steps throughout the TPPM.

Figure 25. Training program planning aid.

Training Program Title

Program Planner _____

Project Team _____

Step	Task	Person Responsible	Target Due Date	Date Completed	Comments
Step 1: Present/Future State Analysis					
Step 2: Program Design					
Step 3: Research					
Step 4: Resource Allocation					
Step 5: Instructional Design					
Step 6: Training Program Instructional Development					
Step 7: Training Program Implementation					
Step 8: Training Program Evaluation					

References

Gronlund, Norman E. *How to Write and Use Instructional Objectives* (5th edition). Englewood Cliffs, NJ: Merrill, 1995.

Hodell, Chuck. "Basics of Instructional Systems Development." *Info-line*. Alexandria, VA: American Society for Training & Development, June 1997.

Kirkpatrick, Donald L. *Evaluating Training Programs*. San Francisco: Berrett-Koehler, 1994.

Kotter, John P. *Leading Change*. Boston: Harvard Business School Press, 1997.

Kotter, John, and John Hesket. *Corporate Culture and Performance*. New York: Free Press, 1992.

Mager, Robert F. *Preparing Instructional Objectives* (2d edition). Belmont, CA: Lake Publishing, 1984.

McCain, Mary L., and Cynthia Pantazis. *Responding to Workplace Change*. Alexandria, VA: American Society for Training & Development, 1997.

Redding, John. "Hardwiring the Learning Organization." *Training & Development*. Alexandria, VA: American Society for Training & Development, August 1997, 61-67.

Rothwell, William J., and Peter S. Cookson. *Beyond Instruction*. San Francisco: Jossey-Bass Publishers, 1997.

Vander Linde, Karen, Nicholas Horney, and Richard Koonce. "Seven Ways to Make Your Training Department One of the Best." *Training & Development*. August 1997, 20-28.

Watson, Scott C. "Five Easy Pieces to Performance Measurement." *Training & Development*. May 1998, 45-48.

Other Resources

Managing the Training Function

Ackerson, Jack. "A Top Level Analysis of Training Management Functions." *Journal of Interactive Instruction Development*. Warrenton, VA: Learning Technology Institute, Summer 1995, 3-6.

Arthur, Diane. *Managing Human Resources in Small and Mid-Sized Companies*. New York: AMACOM, 1995.

Barkley, Bruce T., and James H. Saylor. *Customer-Driven Project Management: A New Paradigm in Total Quality Implementation*. New York: McGraw-Hill, 1994.

Barr, Robert B., and John Tagg. "From Teaching to Learning." *Change*. November/December 1995, 13-25.

Bassi, Laurie J., George Benson, and Scott Cheney. "Position Yourself for the Future." *Training & Development*. Alexandria, VA: American Society for Training & Development, November 1996, 27-42.

Bassi, Laurie J., and Mark E. Van Buren. "The 1998 ASTD State of the Industry Report." *Training & Development*. January 1998, 21-43.

Cohen, Sacha. "Big Ideas for Trainers in Small Companies." *Training & Development*. Alexandria, VA: American Society for Training & Development, April 1998, 26-30.

Darraugh, Barbara (editor). "Understanding Reengineering: Organizational Transformation." *Info-line*. Alexandria, VA: American Society for Training & Development, August 1993.

Dell, Jay, John Fox, and Ralph Malcolm. "Training Situation Analysis: Conducting a Needs Analysis for Teams and New Systems." *Performance Improvement*. Washington, D.C.: International Society for Performance Improvement, March 1998, 18-21.

Eidgahy, Saeid Y. "Management of Diverse HRD Programs: Challenges and Opportunities." *Manage*. Dayton, OH: National Management Association, February 1995, 15-19.

Gayeski, Diane M. "Out-of-the-Box Instructional Design." *Training & Development.* Alexandria, VA: American Society for Training & Development, April 1998, 36-40.

Hale, Judith. "Evaluation: It's Time to Go Beyond Levels 1, 2, 3, and 4." *Performance Improvement.* Washington, DC: International Society for Performance Improvement, February 1998, 30-34.

"Industry Report 1997." *Training.* Minneapolis: Lakewood Publications, October 1997, 33-75.

Kemp, Jerrold E., Gary R. Morrison, and Steven M. Ross. *Designing Effective Instruction* (2d edition). Upper Saddle River, NJ: Merrill, 1998.

Laird, Dugan. *Approaches to Training and Development* (2d edition). New York: Addison-Wesley, 1985.

Lee, Chris. "The Adult Learner: Neglected No More." *Training.* Minneapolis: Lakewood Publications, March 1998, 47-52.

Lucadamo, Lisa, and Scott Cheney. "Learning from the Best." *Training & Development.* Alexandria, VA: American Society for Training & Development, July 1997, 25-28.

McCoy, Carol Prescott. *IN ACTION: Managing the Small Training Staff.* Alexandria, VA: American Society for Training & Development, 1998.

McCullough, Richard C. "Make or Buy: How to Decide." *Info-line.* Alexandria, VA: American Society for Training and Development, October 1988.

McDermott, Brian. *Managing the Training Function Book One: Trends, Politics and Political Issues.* Minneapolis: Lakewood Publications, 1990.

————*Managing the Training Function: Book II.* Minneapolis: Lakewood Publications, 1990.

McKeachie, Wilbert J. *Teaching Tips* (9th edition). Lexington, MA: D.C. Heath, 1994.

Moore, Tony. "Training Tips for Managers." *Performance & Instruction.* Washington, DC: International Society for Performance Improvement, May/June 1996, 10-11.

Nilson, Carolyn. *How to Manage Training: A Guide to Design and Delivery for High Performance* (2d edition). New York: AMACOM, 1997.

Peak, Martha. "Training: No Longer for the Fainthearted." *Management Review.* New York: American Management Association, February 1997, 23-27.

Pepper, Allan. *Managing the Training and Development Function* (2d edition). Brookfield, VT: Ashgate Publishing, 1992.

Powers, Bob. *Instructor Excellence: Mastering the Delivery of Training.* San Francisco: Jossey-Bass Publishers, 1992.

Robinson, Dana Gaines, and James C. Robinson.*Training for Impact: How to Link Training to Business Needs and Measure the Results.* San Francisco: Jossey-Bass Publishers, 1989.

Rothwell, Willam J. *Beyond Training and Development: State-of-the-Art Strategies for Enhancing Human Performance.* New York: AMACOM, 1996.

Rothwell, William J., and Peter S. Cookson. *Beyond Instruction: Comprehensive Program Planning for Business and Education.* San Francisco: Jossey-Bass Publishers, 1997.

Shaw, Edward. *The Six Pillars of Reality-Based Training: A Practical Guide to Designing and Delivering Training that Works.* Minneapolis: Lakewood Publications, 1997.

Smith, Barry J., and Brian L. Delahaye. *How to Be an Effective Trainer: Skills for Managers and New Trainers.* New York: John Wiley & Sons, 1998.

"When Training Fails, Blame Somebody Else, or—Gasp!" *Training Directors' Forum Newsletter,* Minneapolis: Lakewood Publications, April 1998, 4-5.

Wiggenhorn, William A., and Robert L. Craig (editors). *The ASTD Training and Development Handbook: A Guide to Human Resource Development.* New York: McGraw-Hill, 1996.

"Workplace 2006 Trends," *Term/Technical Education Resource Monitor.* Atlanta: Atlanta Information Services, January–February 1998, 2.

Zemke, Ron. "How to Do a Needs Assessment When You Think You Don't Have Time." *Training.* Minneapolis: Lakewood Publications, March 1998.

Planning and Project Management

Bailey, Harold J., and Kathleen A. Ergott. "Project Management: Part 1—The Soft Skills." *Journal of Instruction Delivery Systems.* Warrenton, VA: Learning Technology Institute, Winter 1998, 3-7.

Burke, Rory. *Project Management: Planning and Control.* New York: John Wiley & Sons, 1994.

Conkright, Tom D. "So You're Going to Manage a Project . . ." *Training.* Minneapolis: Lakewood Publications, January 1998, 62-67.

DeFillippi, Robert J., and Michael B. Arthur. "Paradox in Project-Based Enterprise: The Case of Film Making." *California Management Review.* Berkeley, CA: University of California, Berkeley, Winter 1998, 125-139.

DeWeaver, Mary Feeherry, and Lori Ciprian Gillespie. *Real-World Project Management: New Approaches for Adapting to Change and Uncertainty.* New York: Quality Resources, 1997.

Dickson, Ron. "How to Salvage a Sunken Project." *Training & Development,* Alexandria, VA: American Society for Training & Development, December 1995, 12-13.

Dinsmore, Paul C. (editor). *The AMA Handbook of Project Management.* New York: AMACOM, 1993.

Forsberg, Kevin, Hal Mooz, and Howard Cotterman. *Visualizing Project Management.* New York: John Wiley & Sons, 1996.

Fuller, Jim. *Managing Performance Improvement Projects: Preparing, Planning, and Implementing.* San Francisco: Jossey-Bass Publishers, 1997.

Greer, Michael. "Essential Skills for Today's 'Instant' Project Managers." *Performance Improvement.* Washington, DC: International Society for Performance Improvement, February 1998, 24-29.

Layng, Jacqueline. "Parallels Between Project Management and Instructional Design." *Performance Improvement.* Washington, DC: International Society for Performance Improvement, July 1997, 16-20.

Lewis, James P. *Fundamentals of Project Management (The Worksmart).* New York: AMACOM, 1995.

Pokras, Sandy. *Rapid Team Deployment: Building High Performance Project Teams.* Menlo Park, CA: Crisp Publications, 1995.

Stamps, David. "Lights, Camera, Project Management!" *Training.* Minneapolis: Lakewood Publications, January 1997, 50-56.

Stevens, Larry. "The Right Mix." *Human Resource Executive,* Horsham, PA: LRP Magazine Group, April 1997, 52-56.

Thornley, James. "Tips for Project Management." *Performance & Instruction.* Washington, DC: International Society for Performance Improvement, May/June 1996, 6-8.

Weiss, Joseph W., and Robert K. Wysocki. *5-Phase Project Management: A Practical Planning & Implementation Guide.* New York: Addison-Wesley, 1992.

Wysocki, Robert K.; Beck, Robert; and David B. Crane. *Effective Project Management: How to Plan, Manage, and Deliver Projects on Time and Within Budget.* New York: John Wiley & Sons, 1995.

Critical Thinking Skills in Decision Making

Arnold, John D. *The Complete Problem Solver: A Total System for Competitive Decision Making.* New York: John Wiley & Sons, 1992.

Benner, Patricia Ann. *Breakthroughs in Critical Reading: Developing Reading and Critical Thinking Skills.* Lincolnwood, IL: NTC/Contemporary Publishing, 1996.

Brookfield, Stephen D. "Assessing Critical Thinking." *Directions for Adult and Continuing Education.* San Francisco: Jossey-Bass Publishers, Fall 1997, 17-29.

Cammarano, Roy F., and James J. Cammarano. *6 Steps to Effective Decision Making: A Process to Ensure Optimum Result.* Glendale, CA: Griffin Publishing, 1998.

Garrison, D.R. "Critical Thinking and Self-Directed Learning in Adult Education: An Analysis of Responsibility and Control Issues." *Adult Education Quarterly.* Washington, DC: American Association for Adult & Continuing Education, Spring 1992, 136-148.

Hale, Guy A. *The Leader's Edge: Mastering the Five Skills of Breakthrough Thinking.* Burr Ridge, IL: Irwin Professional Publishing, 1995.

Kaplan, Robert S., and David P. Norton. "Using the Balanced Scorecard as a Strategic Management System." *Harvard Business Review.* Cambridge, MA: Harvard Business School, January–February 1996.

Keeney, Ralph L. *Value-Focused Thinking: A Path to Creative Decisionmaking.* Cambridge, MA: Harvard University Press, 1996.

Kramlinger, Tom. "How to Deliver a Change Message." *Training & Development.* Alexandria, VA: American Society for Training & Development, April 1998.

Little, Linda W., and Ingrid A. Greenberg. *Problem Solving: Critical Thinking and Communication Skills.* United Kingdom: Longman Group, 1991.

Schoemaker, Paul J.H. "Scenario Planning: A Tool for Strategic Thinking." *Sloan Management Review.* Cambridge, MA: MIT Sloan School of Management, Winter 1995, 25-40.

Schwenk, Charles R. "Strategic Decision Making." *Journal of Management.* Greenwich, CT: JAI Press, volume 21, 1995, 471-493.

Senge, Peter. *The Fifth Discipline Fieldbook.* New York: Doubleday, 1994.

Spitzer, Quinn, and Ron Evans. "The New Business Leader: Socrates with a Baton." *Strategy & Leadership.* Chicago, IL: Strategic Leadership Forum, September/October 1997, 32-38.

————"Putting It in Play." *Human Resource Executive.* Horsham, PA: LRP Magazine Group, February 1997, 43-45.

Budget Management

"10 Ways to Stretch Your Budget, But Keep Training Quality High." *Training Directors' Forum Newsletter.* Minneapolis: Lakewood Publications, January 1996, 7.

Allerton, Haidee. "What Things Cost." *Training & Development.* Alexandria, VA: American Society for Training & Development, June 1996, 20-23.

Aloian, Dena C., and William R. Fowler. "How to Create a High-Performance Training Plan." *Training & Development.* Alexandria, VA: American Society for Training & Development, November 1994, 43-44.

Bellman, Geoffrey M. "Trimming Your Waste Line." *Training & Development.* Alexandria, VA: American Society for Training & Development, May 1993, 28-31.

Callahan, Madelyn R. "Training on a Shoestring." *Training & Development.* Alexandria, VA: American Society for Training & Development, December 1995, 18-23.

Craig, Robert L. (editor). *The ASTD Training and Development Handbook: A Guide to Human Resource Development,* New York: McGraw-Hill, 1996.

Head, Glenn E. *Training Cost Analysis: A How-to Guide for Trainers and Managers.* Alexandria, VA: American Society for Training & Development, 1994.

"How to Do More with Less: Practical Ideas for Stretching a Training Budget." *Training Directors' Forum Newsletter.* Minneapolis: Lakewood Publications, December 1996, 1-3.

Nilson, Carolyn. *How to Manage Training: A Guide to Administration, Design, and Delivery.* New York: American Management Association, 1991.

————*Training Program Workbook and Kit.* Englewood Cliffs, NJ: Prentice Hall, 1989.

"Solid Cost Estimates Now Mean Few Surprises Down the Road." *Training Directors' Forum Newsletter.* Minneapolis: Lakewood Publications, October 1992, 5.

Svenson, Raynold A., and Monica J. Rinderer. *The Training and Development Strategic Plan Workbook.* Englewood Cliffs, NJ: Prentice Hall, 1992.

Williams, Paul B. *Getting a Project Done on Time: Managing People, Time, and Results.* New York: AMACOM, 1996.

Wysocki, Robert K., Robert Beck, and David B. Crane. *Effective Project Management: How to Plan, Manage, and Deliver Projects on Time and Within Budget.* New York: John Wiley & Sons, 1995.

The Author

Karen Overfield is vice president of faculty development for the Education Management Corporation. In this position, she works with Art Institutes International, New York Restaurant School, and NCPT (National Center for Professional Training) deans of education to design faculty development programs at the schools, develops systemwide programs for faculty, and serves as an internal resource.

Before joining Education Management Corporation, Overfield was an organizational development and training consultant in the Corporate Organizational Development and Training Department of Bayer Corporation. In that capacity, she served as an internal organizational development consultant; course designer, developer, facilitator; and program manager.

Prior to joining Bayer, Overfield managed the Word Processing Department and served as internal consultant on office automation systems, procedures, and applications at McGraw-Edison's Power Systems Headquarters. There, she served as liaison between corporate staff and the Management Information Systems Department.

In addition, Overfield teaches training and development courses in the Master's of Public Management Program at the H. John Heinz III School of Public Policy and Management of Carnegie-Mellon University. She has taught organizational development at the Joseph M. Katz Graduate School of Business and has taught managing the training function at the International Management Development Institute at the University of Pittsburgh. She has also served on the faculty at Robert Morris College, where she taught at the graduate, undergraduate, and associate degree levels in the Business and Administrative Management Department.

Overfield's articles on training have appeared in the following publications: *P&I, Training & Development, Performance and Instruction, Info-line, THE Journal, Education and Training Exchange, Journal of Business Education, Interface, Words, ESU Business Review,* and *Business Education Forum.* She has also facilitated numerous workshops and given presentations throughout the United States.

Overfield has a B.S. degree in business studies from Carnegie-Mellon University, an M.Ed. in distributive education from the University of Pittsburgh, and an Ed.D. in vocational education and curriculum and supervision from the University of Pittsburgh. She is a member of the American Society for Training & Development (ASTD) and the International Society for Performance and Instruction (ISPI). She is also a member of the board of directors for Auberle. She has served on educational advisory councils and steering committees for the University of Pittsburgh, Robert Morris College, Community College of Allegheny County, Parkway West Technical School, and the Institute of Advanced Technology. She was also a contributing editor for *Education and Training Exchange.*